A PLUME BOOK

TOP SECRET RECIPES UNLOCKED

TODD WILBUR is the bestselling QVC cookbook author. He's appeared on *The Oprah Winfrey Show, Today,* and *Good Morning America,* among others. He lives in Las Vegas.

"These probably come as close as you can get to the original recipes." —*Boston Herald*

"Many of [Wilbur's] dishy imitations come, like a box of Cracker Jacks, with a surprise inside." —*Mademoiselle*

"The recipes are simply written and easy to do. This book offers great-tasting fun for the whole family." —*The Clinton Chronicle* (South Carolina)

"The mission: Decode the secret recipes for America's favorite junk foods. Equipment: Standard kitchen appliances. Goal: Leak the recipes to a ravenous public." —*USA Today*

VISIT US ON THE WEB AT WWW.TOPSECRETRECIPES.COM

ALSO BY TODD WILBUR

Top Secret Recipes

More Top Secret Recipes

Even More Top Secret Recipes

Top Secret Restaurant Recipes

Top Secret Restaurant Recipes 2

Top Secret Recipes Lite!

Low-Fat Top Secret Recipes

Top Secret Recipes: Sodas, Smoothies, Spirits, & Shakes

TOP SECRET RECIPES UNLOCKED

All New Home Clones of America's Favorite Brand-Name Foods

TODD WILBUR

With Illustrations by the Author

A PLUME BOOK

PLUME
Published by the Penguin Group
Penguin Group (USA) Inc., 375 Hudson Street, New York, New York 10014, U.S.A. • Penguin Group
(Canada), 90 Eglinton Avenue East, Suite 700, Toronto, Ontario, Canada M4P 2Y3
(a division of Pearson Penguin Canada Inc.) • Penguin Books Ltd., 80 Strand, London
WC2R 0RL, England • Penguin Ireland, 25 St. Stephen's Green, Dublin 2, Ireland (a division of
Penguin Books Ltd.) • Penguin Group (Australia), 250 Camberwell Road, Camberwell, Victoria
3124, Australia (a division of Pearson Australia Group Pty. Ltd.) • Penguin Books India Pvt. Ltd.,
11 Community Centre, Panchsheel Park, New Delhi–110 017, India • Penguin Group (NZ),
67 Apollo Drive, Rosedale, North Shore 0632, New Zealand (a division of Pearson
New Zealand Ltd.) • Penguin Books (South Africa) (Pty.) Ltd., 24 Sturdee Avenue, Rosebank,
Johannesburg 2196, South Africa

Penguin Books Ltd., Registered Offices: 80 Strand, London WC2R 0RL, England

First published by Plume, a member of Penguin Group (USA) Inc.

First Printing, December 2009
10 9 8 7 6 5 4 3 2 1

LIBRARY OF CONGRESS CATALOGING-IN-PUBLICATION DATA

Wilbur, Todd.
  Top secret recipes unlocked : all new home clones of America's favorite brand-name foods /
Todd Wilbur ; with illustrations by the author.
    p.   cm.
  Includes index.
  ISBN 978-0-452-29579-7 (pbk. : alk. paper) 1. Cookery, American.   2. Chain
restaurants—United States.   I. Title.
    TX715.W65867   2009
    641.5973—dc22   2009025663

Printed in the United States of America

For Morea

CONTENTS

A Little Foreword   xiii

Thank You   xv

Introduction   xvii

Arby's® Horsey Sauce®   1

Baja Fresh® Salsa Baja   2

Bisquick® Original All-Purpose Baking Mix   4

Boston Market® Butternut Squash   6

Boston Market® Garlic Dill New Potatoes   8

Boston Market® Sweet Potato Casserole   11

Budweiser® Chelada   13

Burger King® Onion Rings   14

Burger King® Zesty Onion Ring Sauce   17

Carl's Jr.® The Six Dollar Burger™   18

Carnegie Deli® Classic New York City Cheesecake   21

Chex Mix® Bold Party Blend   24

Chick-fil-A® Honey Roasted BBQ Sauce   27

Chick-fil-A® Carrot and Raisin Salad   29

Chipotle Mexican Grill® Chipotle-Honey Vinaigrette   31

Chipotle Mexican Grill® Barbacoa Burrito   33

CLIFF & BUSTER® COCONUT MACAROONS   38

COCA-COLA® BLĀK®   41

CRUNCH 'N MUNCH® BUTTERY TOFFEE POPCORN WITH PEANUTS   43

DAIRY QUEEN® MOOLATTÉ®   45

DEL TACO® CRISPY FISH TACO   47

DUNCAN HINES® MOIST DELUXE® YELLOW CAKE MIX   50

DUNKIN' DONUTS® COFFEE COOLATTA®   52

EINSTEIN BROS. BAGELS® SANTA FE EGG SANDWICH   54

EL POLLO LOCO® AVOCADO SALSA   56

EL POLLO LOCO® BBQ BLACK BEANS   57

EL POLLO LOCO® CREAMY CILANTRO DRESSING   59

FAMOUS AMOS® CHOCOLATE CHIP COOKIES   60

FRITOS® HOT BEAN DIP   63

HEINZ® PREMIUM CHILI SAUCE   64

HELLMANN'S®/BEST FOODS® MAYONNAISE   66

HIDDEN VALLEY® THE ORIGINAL RANCH® DRESSING   69

JACK IN THE BOX® PUMPKIN PIE SHAKE   71

JACQUIN'S® PEPPERMINT SCHNAPPS   73

JASON'S DELI® CREAMY LIQUEUR FRUIT DIPPING SAUCE   74

JIMMY DEAN® BREAKFAST SAUSAGE   75

    REGULAR   75

    MAPLE   76

    HOT   76

KFC® CAJUN HONEY WINGS   77

KFC® CHICKEN POT PIE   80

KOZY SHACK® RICE PUDDING   84

KRAFT® MIRACLE WHIP®   87

KRISPY KREME® ORIGINAL GLAZED DOUGHNUTS   89

Lawry's® Red Pepper Seasoned Salt (made with Tabasco®)   94

Lipton® Brisk® Iced Tea   96

Lipton® Diet Green Tea with Citrus   97

Lincoln Snacks® Poppycock®   99

Maid-Rite® Loose Meat Sandwich   102

Mars® Munch® Bar   106

Mauna Loa® Kona Coffee Glazed® Macadamias   109

McDonald's® Sweet Tea   112

McDonald's® Vanilla Iced Coffee   113

McDonald's® Cinnamon Melts   115

McDonald's® Fruit & Walnut Salad   119

McDonald's® Tangy Honey Mustard   121

McDonald's® McLobster Sandwich   122

Mrs. Fields® Cranberry White Chocolate Cookies   124

Mrs. Fields® Pumpkin Harvest Cookies   127

No Pudge! ® Original Fat Free Fudge Brownie Mix   130

Nuts 4 Nuts® Candied Nuts   133

Old Bay® Seasoning   135

Orange Julius® Banana Julius   136

Orange Julius® Strawberry-Banana Classic Smoothie   137

Pal's® Sauce Burger®   139

Panera Bread® Broccoli Cheddar Soup   141

Panera Bread® Cranberry Walnut Bagel   143

Panera Bread® French Onion Soup   146

Panera Bread® Spinach Artichoke Baked Egg Soufflé   148

Pepperidge Farm® Soft Baked Snickerdoodle Cookies   152

Popeyes® Buttermilk Biscuits   155

Popeyes® Cajun Gravy   158

POPEYES® CAJUN SPARKLE®   160

POPEYES® RED BEANS & RICE (IMPROVED)   161

RAGÚ® PASTA SAUCES   164

    MEAT   164

       TOMATO, BASIL, AND ITALIAN CHEESE   164

RONDELÉ® GARLIC & HERBS CHEESE SPREAD   166

SABRA® CLASSIC HUMMUS   168

SKYLINE® CHILI   170

SONIC DRIVE-IN® PEANUT BUTTER SHAKE AND

       PEANUT BUTTER FUDGE SHAKE   172

SONIC DRIVE-IN® STRAWBERRY CHEESECAKE SHAKE   173

SONIC DRIVE-IN® SONIC BURGER   175

SONIC DRIVE-IN® HICKORY BURGER   178

SONIC DRIVE-IN® JALAPEÑO BURGER   180

THE SOUP NAZI'S CRAB BISQUE   183

THE SOUP NAZI'S CREAM OF SWEET POTATO SOUP   185

THE SOUP NAZI'S INDIAN MULLIGATAWNY   187

THE SOUP NAZI'S MEXICAN CHICKEN CHILI   189

SPATINI® SPAGHETTI SAUCE MIX   191

STARBUCKS® CARAMEL MACCHIATO   193

STARBUCKS® FRAPPUCCINO® (BOTTLED VERSION)   195

STARBUCKS® GINGERBREAD LATTE   197

STARBUCKS® HOT CHOCOLATE   199

STARBUCKS® MOCHA COCONUT FRAPPUCCINO®   201

STARBUCKS® CARROT CAKE   203

STARBUCKS® CLASSIC COFFEE CAKE   205

STARBUCKS® CRANBERRY BLISS BAR   208

STARBUCKS® LEMON LOAF   211

Starbucks® Maple Oat Nut Scone   214

Starbucks® Peppermint Brownie   217

Starbucks® Pumpkin Bread   220

Starbucks® Pumpkin Cream Cheese Muffin   223

Starbucks® Pumpkin Scone   227

Starbucks® Vanilla Almond Biscotti   231

Stouffer's® Macaroni & Cheese   234

Subway® Bourbon Street Glaze   237

Subway® Chipotle Southwest Sauce   238

Subway® Sweet Onion Sauce   239

Taco Bell® Baja Sauce   240

Taco Bell® Chicken Quesadilla   241

Taco Bell® Mild Border Sauce®   244

Weight Watchers® Smart Ones® Banana Muffins   245

Wendy's® Garden Sensations® Mandarin Chicken Salad   247

Wendy's® Wild Mountain Bacon Cheeseburger   249

Yonah Schimmel Low-Fat New York City Knish   252

Trademarks   255

Index   259

A LITTLE FOREWORD

From *Top Secret Recipes,* 1993

In the laboratory (my kitchen), each of these recipes was subjected to a battering array of bakings and mixings, batch after batch, until the closest representation of the actual commercial product was finally achieved. I did not swipe, heist, bribe, or otherwise obtain any formulas through coercion or illegal means. I'd like to think that many of these recipes are the actual formulas for their counterparts, but there's no way of knowing for sure. In such cases of closely guarded secret recipes, the closer one gets to matching a real product's contents, the less likely it is that the protective manufacturer will say so.

The objective here was to duplicate the taste and texture of the products with everyday ingredients. In most cases, obtaining the exact ingredients for these mass-produced food products is nearly impossible. For the sake of security and convenience, many of the companies have contracted confidentially with vendors for the specialized production and packaging of each of their products' ingredients. These prepackaged mixes and ingredients are then sent directly to the company for final preparation.

Debbi Fields of Mrs. Fields Cookies, for example, arranged with several individual companies to custom manufacture many of her cookies' ingredients. Her vanilla alone is specially blended from a variety of beans grown in various places around the world. The other ingredients—the chocolate, the eggs, the sugars, the flour—all get specialized attention specifically for the Mrs. Fields company. The same holds true for McDonald's, Wendy's, KFC, and most of the big-volume companies.

Even if you could bypass all the security measures and somehow get your hands on the secret formulas, you'd have a hard time executing the recipes without locating many ingredients usually impossible to find at the corner market. Therefore, with taste in mind, substitution of ingredients other than those that may be used in the actual products is necessary in many cases to achieve a closely cloned end result.

THANK YOU

It's not easy to express in words just how grateful I am to everyone who has helped transform a 134-page trade paperback published in 1993 into a continuing series of cookbooks that has sold more than 4 million copies. From the person who plucked that first unsolicited manuscript out of the slush pile at Plume nearly twenty years ago, to the casual cook who uses these books—and to everyone in between—I am so very thankful. As long as delicious new brand-name foods are created, and as long as I am lucky enough to have such a great crew behind the scenes, I hope to continue developing these culinary clones that can make home-cooked foods cool and fun.

Thanks to all at Penguin Group: Clare Ferraro, Cherise Fisher, Barbara O'Shea, Sandra Dear, Kimberly Cagle, Cherisse Landau, and everyone else who has tossed a pinch of this and a dash of that into these books over the years.

Thanks to the awesome hosts at QVC: Jill Bauer, Bob Bower-sox, Jayne Brown, Rick Domeier, Carolyn Gracie, Dan Hughes, Dave James, Pat James-DeMentri, Lisa Mason, Lisa Robertson, Mary Beth Roe, Jane Tracey, David Venable, Dan Wheeler, Leah Williams, and all of the QVC buyers, planners, and producers.

Thanks to Robert Reynolds, Bill Brucker, Perry Rogers, Robert John Kley, Darren Emmens, Malena Gibaja, and MeLinda Baca for their contributions, assistance, and advice.

Thanks to everyone at the *Howard Stern Show* for always keeping me entertained during those long hours in the kitchen. Bonus points: If Howard hadn't ended up on the radio, he says he would have been a chef.

Thanks to Anthony Corrado (a man who works even better without sleep), for always making the food look so delicious in photos and on TV. He's a master at turning the hard work into a really good time.

Thanks to my family and friends, for stepping up as willing and honest taste-test guinea pigs. You didn't have to eat that really gross one, but you did anyway.

And a huge thanks (with a hug and a kiss) to my dearest critic and supporter, Pamela. She's the secret ingredient behind everything that I have created, including my most cherished reproduction yet— my little daughter, Morea.

INTRODUCTION

In his hilarious *Raw* stand-up special from 1987, Eddie Murphy tells a story about when he was a kid begging his mother for a McDonald's hamburger.

"I'll make you a hamburger *better* than McDonald's," she tells him.

"Better than McDonald's?"

"That's right. And you can help Momma make it. Now go get that big black frying pan under the stove. And go to the fridge and get me the chopped meat, and while you're in there get a green pepper and an onion."

Eddie is confused. "But there ain't no green pepper in McDonald's."

"I need a green pepper and an onion, and while you're in there get me an egg out too."

Now Eddie is even more confused. "What you need eggs for? I want a hamburger. You're making an Egg McMuffin!"

"I'm not makin' an Egg McMuffin. I don't even know what a damn Egg McMuffin is. Just get me the egg out and shut your mouth."

He then describes how his mom takes the egg and mixes it with the meat and big chunks of green pepper and paprika and a bunch of other crazy stuff, and then she makes a giant meatball out of it and slaps it down into the hot frying pan, and it starts cooking.

Eddie is disgusted. "There's a big split in the middle and grease is popping out, and you're looking at it while it's poppin' and you're thinking to yourself, 'That don't look like no McDonald's!' "

Eddie's right, of course. That burger didn't look like anything from McDonald's, and it surely didn't taste like anything from McDonald's, unless the chain starts to sell a McGreasy Green Pepper Paprika Meatball Sandwich.

Little Eddie was able to tell right away that Momma's burger was going to be a bad McDonald's clone, even before tasting it, because he knows what a McDonald's hamburger looks like . . . and what it shouldn't look like. Momma's clone was obviously way off, but knowing which recipes are going to work and which ones aren't isn't always that easy. I have seen many so-called copycat recipes created by people with very little kitchen experience, and dubious intentions—the recipes are poorly designed, ingredients have been tossed together without any analysis or testing, and then a brand name is slapped on top. What's up with that? A "copycat" recipe, at first glance, might *seem* to make sense. It's not till you and your bummed-out crew take the first bite that you realize you've been duped. The end result is big waste of time, and a waste of the money you spent on all the ingredients. Oh well. Crank up the garbage disposal. Call in the dog.

Making good clone recipes takes time—a lot of time. Ingredients are tactfully added and subtracted from every attempt, measurements must be carefully reevaluated, and cooking times and temperatures are incrementally adjusted with each new batch. It's a procedure that requires significant trial and error, and most of what I make every day ends up in the can or down the drain. I suspect no one else writes clone recipe cookbooks from scratch for a living because it's such an expensive and tedious process.

Way before the cooking starts I spend a lot of time deciding which brand-name foods to duplicate. From the e-mail link on our Web site, www.TopSecretRecipes.com, I receive hundreds of new cloning suggestions each week. These e-mail requests are logged, and then I use that list to build each *Top Secret Recipes* volume. I try to clone only the most popular and most widely available products, and this list is the best way I know to find out which recipes you want.

The next step involves finding out everything I can about the original product. If it's an item from a restaurant chain, I will talk to servers in each restaurant to get important information about how the dishes are prepared. Ingredients lists on packaged products or on fast-food chain Web sites provide many pieces of the puzzle for those particular clones. I can also get a lot of information about how dishes are made by simply peering into the kitchens or behind the counters where preparation is on display.

Designing a clone recipe may sometimes require extreme measures, such as when I was creating the recipe for Salsa Baja from Baja Fresh (page 2). The recipe wasn't as easy to create as I first thought. I assumed the tomatoes would have to be blackened over a hot grill, but I wasn't sure how to get them black enough to turn the salsa as dark a color as the original without the tomatoes getting all mushy and falling apart on the grill. I went to Baja Fresh before they opened and looked through the window to see if I could catch some hot salsa-making action. I waited and waited. The restaurant had now opened, yet after a couple of hours, as the lunch rush was beginning to wind down, there was still no fresh salsa in the pipeline. I decided it was time to make a move that would get things rolling, so I went up to the counter and ordered 30 tubs of Salsa Baja to go. The restaurant immediately went into "Salsa Baja Red Alert" to replenish the now-dwindling salsa reserve. As I was paying for my giant bag of salsa tubs, a cook came out from the refrigerator with a huge box of tomatoes and tossed them onto the hot grill. Ah-ha! That's when I discovered that the tomatoes should be cold and not too ripe. I watched the entire cooking process from a nearby hi-top, and got all the information I needed to make a perfect clone recipe that day . . . plus 2 gallons of Salsa Baja to go.

Most of the time I don't have the luxury of eyewitnessing the cooking process. Usually I must design a recipe from scratch with just a little information, cook it up once, and then start sculpting from there. After the first batch, I will run a side-by-side taste-test comparison between the clone and the original and determine what needs to be changed. This is often a race against the clock, especially with freshly prepared foods. No matter how well the food is sealed up, the flavors, colors, and textures of the dish are changing with every hour that ticks away. You know how the leftovers in the doggie bag never taste the same as they did the night before at the restaurant? The time factor certainly makes my job more challenging. Once I feel that a finished clone recipe is done, I will go back to the restaurant to get an additional serving of the dish and run another comparison using the fresher new sample just to be sure it's on track.

Analyzing a famous food may require a number of tricks and techniques. My fine-mesh strainer has always been a great tool to help determine what solid ingredients are used in sauces, and for years I've been chilling dishes to see how much fat separates from the rest of the ingredients. Smelling and squeezing and smearing foods have long been habits in my underground lab.

Regardless of the techniques I employ, the end result will always be a culinary carbon copy that you can easily follow, using common ingredients from your local grocery store, and without the need for any commercial kitchen equipment. When you use these recipes to re-create these dishes at home you get to enjoy the taste of your favorite foods at a fraction of the cost of the real thing. And now that you have complete control over what goes into each and every dish you duplicate you can customize any formula to suit your specific preferences and dietary requirements.

There are a wide variety of what I call "convenience foods" in this *Top Secret Recipes* volume; many famous comfort foods that have been on my master "To-Do" list for a long time, such as Kozy Shack Rice Pudding (page 84), Stouffer's Macaroni & Cheese (page 234), Maid-Rite Loose Meat Sandwich (page 102), and Skyline Chili (page 170).

You'll also find many recipes here for re-creating your favorite items from quick-service chains. A clone recipe for the amazing Barbacoa Burrito from Chipotle Mexican Grill is included (page 33), along with Burger King Onion Rings (page 14), Carl's Jr. Six Dollar Burger (page 18), and the Boston Market Sweet Potato Casserole (page 11), which makes an awesome holiday side dish.

You'll also find a great collection of clones for your favorite famous pastries in this volume, including Krispy Kreme Original Glazed Doughnuts (page 89), McDonald's Cinnamon Melts (page 115), and the secret technique for making New York–style cheesecake just as they do at Carnegie Deli (page 21). There are even a whopping ten recipes for cloning the most popular and most requested Starbucks pastries! You're bound to have a favorite among these babies.

Having a collection of clones like this guarantees that the tastes of food you love will live on forever—even when the original product is no longer available. There are several recipes in this book that will show you how to resurrect tastes that are no longer with us. KFC

Cajun Honey Wings (page 77), Wendy's Wild Mountain Bacon Cheeseburger smothered with the great Southwestern Pepper Sauce (page 249), and Coca-Cola Blāk (page 41) may be gone from stores, but the recipes in this book will bring them back to life in your own kitchen. You'll even find a simple formula for Spatini Spaghetti Sauce Mix (page 191) that was sold in stores for more than forty years before Lawry's discontinued it in 2006. I bought a box of the stuff off of eBay, replicated it, and now you can make it for yourself anytime you like.

I hope you have fun with these recipes and blow everyone away with your new ability to duplicate your favorite famous foods. I write these books so that you'll have a great time in the kitchen when you decide to do some cooking. Then, the next time you taste something great and say to yourself, "Man, I wish I could make this at home," you'll know you can. Get yourself some *Top Secret Recipes*, gather around the kitchen, and get on with the cloning!

ARBY'S HORSEY SAUCE

Even though Arby's has diversified its menu over the years with toasted subs and deli-style sandwiches on sliced whole wheat bread, it's the thinly sliced roast beef piled high on hamburger buns that originally made this chain famous. Since roast beef and horseradish go so beautifully together, Arby's created this delicious mayo-based horseradish sauce as a spread for the roast beef sandwiches. It also happens to be great on your homemade sandwiches too, but it just isn't cool to hoard handfuls of those blister packs to take home with you. So, with the help of this secret formula, you can clone as much Horsey Sauce as you want. First step: Get out the blender. You'll need it to puree the horseradish into the mix so that the sauce is smooth and creamy like the real deal.

1 tablespoon white vinegar
4 teaspoons granulated sugar
⅛ teaspoon salt

1 cup mayonnaise
2 tablespoons plus 2 teaspoons
   prepared horseradish

1. In a small dish, dissolve the sugar and salt in the vinegar.
2. Measure the mayonnaise and horseradish into a blender. Add the vinegar solution, and then fire up the blender to medium speed for about 10 seconds, or until the sauce is smooth.
3. Pour the sauce into a container, cover, and chill it for at least a couple of hours to let the flavors get happy.

- MAKES 1 CUP.

BAJA FRESH
SALSA BAJA

You won't find freezers, can openers, or microwave ovens at this national Mexican food chain. Since 1990 Baja Fresh has been serving up great food, made fresh with each order. As you're waiting for your food to come out, that's when you hit up the salsa bar, where you'll find several varieties of delicious fresh salsa, from hot to mild, ready to be spooned into little tubs that you can take to your table or to your car. One of the most popular selections is called Salsa Baja: Its medium spiciness, smoky flavor, and deep black color make the salsa unique and mysterious. That is, until now, since I've got a Top Secret formula for you right here. Blacken the tomatoes and jalapeños on your grill, then dump all the ingredients into a blender. Now you're just a button press away from 3 cups of amazing homemade salsa.

7 firm medium tomatoes, cold
2 jalapeño peppers
1 clove garlic
1 teaspoon salt
1 ½ cups water

juice of 1 lime
2 tablespoons diced white onion
2 tablespoons chopped fresh
   cilantro

1. Preheat the barbecue grill to high heat.
2. Place 6 of the tomatoes, stem-side-down (remove any stems), directly on the grill. Roast the tomatoes over the flame for 10 to 20 minutes. When the tomatoes are very charred and blackened on the first side, flip them over and continue to grill for another 10 to 20 minutes, until most of the surface of each tomato is black. When you flip over the tomatoes, add the jalapeños to

the grill (take the stem off first). The jalapeño skin will blacken like the tomatoes. Turn the peppers as they cook so that all the skin darkens.

3. Take the tomatoes and peppers off the grill and put them in a bowl to cool for 10 to 15 minutes. Dump the tomatoes and peppers and any liquid in the bowl into a blender. Add the garlic and salt and blend on high speed until pureed. Add the water and lime juice and blend again on high speed for 30 to 45 seconds. As the blackened bits of tomato are chopped finer, the sauce will darken.

4. Pour the mixture into a bowl. Dice the remaining tomato and add it to the salsa. Add the onion and cilantro, then let the salsa cool in the refrigerator.

- MAKES 3 CUPS.

• • • •

BISQUICK ORIGINAL
ALL-PURPOSE BAKING MIX

You've got a hankerin' for pancakes or biscuits, but the recipe calls for Bisquick and you're plum out. Not to worry. Now you can make a clone of the popular baking mix at home with just four simple ingredients. Store-bought Bisquick includes shortening, salt, flour, and leavening, so that's exactly what we need to duplicate it perfectly at home. This recipe makes about 6 cups of the stuff, which, just like the real thing, you can keep sealed up in a container in your pantry until it's flapjack time. When that time comes, just add milk and eggs for pancakes or waffles, or only milk if it's biscuits you want. You'll find all those recipes below in Tidbits.

4 cups all-purpose flour	*1 ½ teaspoons salt*
2 tablespoons baking powder	*1 cup shortening*

1. Combine all the dry ingredients in a large bowl.
2. Add the shortening and mix with an electric mixer on medium speed until all the shortening is blended with the flour.
3. Use the mix as you would the real thing by following the directions on the box (see Tidbits below).

- MAKES 6 CUPS.

Tidbits
Use the following recipes to make pancakes, waffles, and biscuits with the cloned version of the mix as you would with the real thing:

Pancakes

Stir 2 cups Bisquick clone mix with 1 cup milk and 2 eggs in a bowl until blended. Pour ¼ cup portions onto a hot griddle and cook until the edges are dry. Turn; cook until golden on the other side. Makes 14 pancakes.

Waffles

Stir 2 cups Bisquick clone mix with 1⅓ cups milk, 1 egg, and 2 tablespoons vegetable oil in a bowl until blended. Pour onto a hot waffle iron and bake until the steaming stops. Makes twelve 4-inch waffles.

Biscuits

Preheat the oven to 450 degrees F. Stir 2¼ cups Bisquick clone mix with ⅔ cup milk. When a dough forms, turn it out onto a surface and sprinkle with extra mix. Knead 10 times. Roll the dough ¼ inch thick and cut with a 2½-inch cutter. Place on an ungreased cookie sheet. Bake for 8 to 10 minutes, or until golden brown. Makes 9 biscuits.

• • • •

BOSTON MARKET
BUTTERNUT SQUASH

☆ ✌ 💣 ✏ ☯ ✂ ☞

Here's a technique for making flavorful butternut squash that's crazy easy. Most of your time will be spent cutting the squash into 1-inch cubes so that you can steam it. Use a sharp peeler to remove the tough skin, then skip on over to the chopping block (but please, no skipping with a sharp knife). You can alternately use a microwave to cook the squash whole (see Tidbits), although I prefer the texture from good old-fashioned steaming. After the squash is cooked, mash it up, mix in the other ingredients, and you've got a great side that fits right in with many meals, especially spicy dishes. Since this squash comes in varying sizes, you may want to start with just ¼ teaspoon of salt, give it a taste, then add more to suit you and your buds.

1 medium butternut squash
2 tablespoons butter, melted
2 tablespoons light brown sugar
½ teaspoon salt

¼ teaspoon ground nutmeg
¼ teaspoon ground allspice
⅛ teaspoon ground black pepper

1. Cut the squash into quarters. Remove the seeds and slice off the skin, then chop the squash into 1-inch cubes. Put the squash in a steamer rack in a large saucepan over boiling water and cover. Steam for 30 minutes, or until the squash is tender.

2. When the squash has cooked, use a potato masher to mash the squash until smooth in a large bowl. Add the remaining ingredients and continue mashing until everything is mixed in. Let the squash sit for at least 10 minutes so that the flavors can mingle. Reheat in the microwave for a minute or so before serving.

- MAKES 4 SERVINGS.

Tidbits

If you want to cook the squash in the microwave, poke several deep slices in the whole squash with a paring knife. Microwave the squash on high for 20 minutes, or until you see all of the tough outer skin change color. The entire surface of the squash should be tender. Let it cool for 15 minutes, then slice it in half and scoop out the seeds with an ice-cream scoop. Toss those, then scoop the good stuff into a bowl and proceed with the recipe from step #2.

• • • •

BOSTON MARKET
GARLIC DILL NEW POTATOES

☆ ✌ 💣 ✏ ☯ ✂ ☞

Technically speaking, "new potatoes" can be any young potato. Boston Market, however, uses red potatoes for this particular dish, and they're actually not all that young. So, for this recipe you need some common, medium-size red potatoes. After cutting the potatoes into bite-size slices, you simply steam them on a steamer rack or basket in a large covered saucepan over boiling water. When the potatoes are done, toss them with a delicious mix of melted butter, fresh dill, and garlic, and you've got a quick clone that could stand up to any taste test.

8 medium red potatoes
3 tablespoons butter, melted
1 tablespoon chopped fresh dill

2 teaspoons minced garlic (about
  2 cloves)
¼ teaspoon salt

1. Cut the potatoes in half (lengthwise), cut the halves in half (also lengthwise), then cut the quarters in half (yeah, still lengthwise), so that you have eight wedges from each potato. Steam the sliced potatoes on a steamer rack over boiling water in a large covered saucepan for 10 minutes, or until the tip of a knife encounters just a little resistance when stuck into the potatoes. The potatoes will cook a bit more after they come off the heat, so you want to be sure not to overcook them.
2. Combine the melted butter, dill, garlic, and salt in a small bowl.

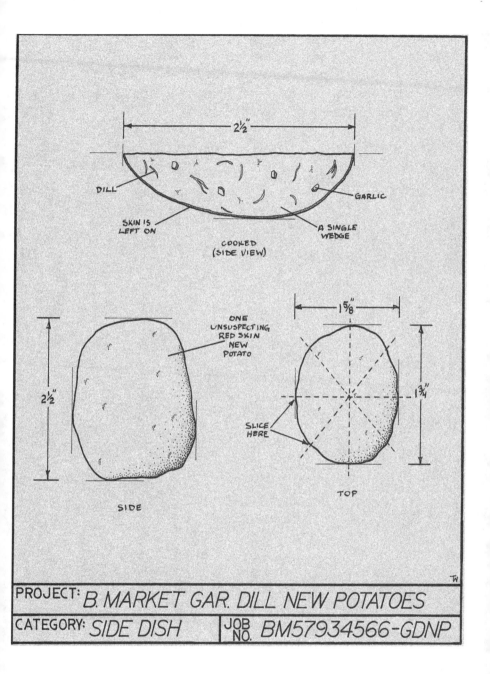

2½"

DILL

GARLIC

SKIN IS
LEFT ON

A SINGLE
WEDGE

COOKED
(SIDE VIEW)

ONE
UNSUSPECTING
RED SKIN
NEW
POTATO

1⅝"

2½"

1¾"

SLICE
HERE

SIDE

TOP

PROJECT: *B. MARKET GAR. DILL NEW POTATOES*

CATEGORY: *SIDE DISH*   JOB NO. *BM57934566-GDNP*

9

3. When the potatoes are cooked, dump them into a medium bowl. Pour the garlic butter over the potatoes, then gently toss the potatoes until they are well coated. Be careful not to toss the potatoes too much or they may start to fall apart, and you're not making mashed potatoes.

- MAKES 4 TO 6 SERVINGS.

•   •   •   •

BOSTON MARKET
SWEET POTATO CASSEROLE

☆   ✌   💣   ✐   ☯   ✂   ☞

This popular pick from Boston Market may be called a side dish, but it tastes more like dessert. With the brown sugar, cinnamon, and butter in there, and the oatmeal streusel on top, you will be reminded of sweet potato pie; yet the dish goes great alongside meals as varied as low-key chicken dinners or bigger-key holiday banquets. And the great part is, if you're planning to use this for entertaining, you can make everything but the streusel a day ahead so you won't be stressed at crunch time. Just cover the filled baking dish and pop it in the fridge. Take it out a few hours before you plan to bake it so the casserole can come close to room temperature, then you simply top it off with your streusel and pop the whole thing in the oven.

6 cups mashed sweet potatoes (5 to 6 potatoes—see step #1)	¼ cup melted butter
	¼ teaspoon ground cinnamon
¾ cup dark brown sugar	¼ teaspoon salt
½ cup heavy cream	2 cups mini marshmallows

OATMEAL STREUSEL

¼ cup rolled oats	⅛ teaspoon ground cinnamon
2 tablespoons dark brown sugar	2 tablespoons cold butter
1 tablespoon all-purpose flour	

1. To make the sweet potatoes, place them on a baking sheet and pop them into a preheated 400 degree F oven for 60 to 70 minutes, or until they are tender. When the potatoes are cool enough to handle, scrape out the insides and use an electric

mixer on high speed to beat the potatoes until they are mashed and smooth. Measure exactly 6 cups of the mashed sweet potatoes into a large bowl.

2. Add the brown sugar, heavy cream, melted butter, cinnamon, and salt to the sweet potatoes and mix well with the beater until all the ingredients are incorporated. Pour this mixture into an 8 x 8-inch baking dish.

3. Now set the oven to 350 degrees F.

4. Make the oatmeal streusel by grinding the rolled oats to a coarse flour using a food processor. Make sure there are still visible bits of oats in there. A blender will also work.

5. Combine the oat flour with the brown sugar, flour, and cinnamon in a small bowl. Cut the cold butter into the dry mixture using a pastry knife or a fork. You should have a crumbly mixture with pea-size bits. Sprinkle this oatmeal streusel over the sweet potato mixture and pop it into the oven for 50 to 60 minutes, or until the top begins to brown slightly.

6. When you remove the casserole from the oven, immediately spread the marshmallows over the top. Let this sit for about 10 minutes. The heat from the casserole will melt the marshmallows, and then it's ready to serve.

- MAKES 6 TO 8 SERVINGS.

• • • •

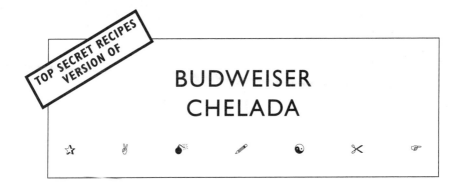

BUDWEISER CHELADA

If you've never had a Chelada, the idea of mixing beer with Clamato juice may make your stomach turn. This odd combination of beverages has origins in Mexico that date back to the 1940s, when beer was mixed with lime, salt, and hot sauce or salsa. In early 2008, Anheuser-Busch (Budweiser) and Cadbury Schweppes (Clamato) teamed up to produce the first canned Chelada beverage, which they dubbed "The Red One," and after a successful launch in select western states, the product is now exploding across the country. Many swear by the drink as a remarkable hangover cure, and after some extensive personal experimentation, I must concur.

12 ounces cold Budweiser beer
¾ cup cold Clamato juice
½ teaspoon lime juice

1 drop Tabasco sauce
1 drop Worcestershire sauce
pinch salt

Combine all the ingredients in an 18-ounce glass or small pitcher, stir gently, and serve.

- MAKES 1 SERVING.

• • • •

BURGER KING
ONION RINGS

Since McDonald's doesn't sell onion rings, these crunchy, golden hoops from the world's number two restaurant chain are the most popular onion rings in the world. There are more than 12,000 Burger Kings in 61 countries these days, and after french fries, onion rings are the second-most popular companion to the chain's signature Whopper sandwich. Check out how simple it is to clone a whopping four dozen onion rings from one onion, using this triple-breading process. When frying, trans-fat-free vegetable shortening makes for the best clone, but you can get by fine using vegetable oil if that's the way you want to go. Check out the next recipe to clone the Zesty Onion Ring Dipping Sauce for adding a little zing to your rings.

6 to 10 cups vegetable shortening (or vegetable oil)	2 cups all-purpose flour
1 medium white onion	2 cups Progresso plain bread crumbs
2 cups milk	salt

1. In a fryer, heat up 6 to 10 cups of vegetable shortening or oil (use the amount required by your fryer) to 350 degrees F.
2. Cut the onion into ¼-inch-thick slices, then separate the slices into rings.
3. Pour the milk into a large shallow bowl, dump flour into another large shallow bowl, and pour bread crumbs into a third large shallow bowl. The large shallow bowls will make breading easier. Easy is good.
4. While the shortening is heating up, bread all the onion rings: First

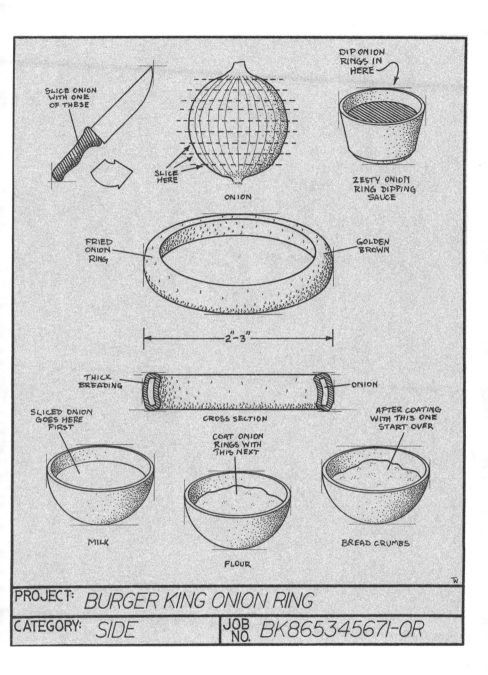

SLICE ONION WITH ONE OF THESE

SLICE HERE

ONION

DIP ONION RINGS IN HERE

ZESTY ONION RING DIPPING SAUCE

FRIED ONION RING

GOLDEN BROWN

2"-3"

THICK BREADING

ONION

CROSS SECTION

SLICED ONION GOES HERE FIRST

COAT ONION RINGS WITH THIS NEXT

AFTER COATING WITH THIS ONE START OVER

MILK

FLOUR

BREAD CRUMBS

PROJECT: *BURGER KING ONION RING*

CATEGORY: *SIDE*

JOB NO. *BK865345671-OR*

dip an onion ring into the milk, then into the flour. Dip it back into the milk, then into the bread crumbs, and once more into the milk and into the bread crumbs. This will give each of the rings a nice thick breading. Arrange the breaded rings on a plate until all of them are breaded.

5. When the oil is hot, fry the rings, a handful at a time, in the oil for 1½ to 3 minutes, or until golden brown. Remove the rings from the oil to a rack or paper towels to drain. Lightly salt the onion rings and serve 'em up hot.

• MAKES 4 TO 5 DOZEN ONION RINGS.

•   •   •   •

BURGER KING
ZESTY ONION RING SAUCE

☆   ✌   💣   ✎   ☯   ✂   ☞

If you're a big fan of onion rings from Burger King, you probably already know about the spicy dipping sauce offered from the world's number two burger chain (it's not always on the menu, and you usually have to request it). The creamy, mayo-based sauce seems to be inspired by the dipping sauce served with Outback's signature Bloomin' Onion appetizer, since both sauces contain similar ingredients, among them horseradish and cayenne pepper. If you're giving the clone for Burger King Onion Rings a try, whip up some of this sauce and go for a dip. It's just as good with low-fat mayonnaise if you're into that. And the stuff works real well as a spread for burgers and sandwiches or for dipping artichokes.

¹/₂ cup mayonnaise
1 ¹/₂ teaspoons ketchup
1 ¹/₂ teaspoons prepared
  horseradish

¹/₂ teaspoon granulated sugar
¹/₂ teaspoon lemon juice
¹/₄ teaspoon cayenne pepper

Combine all the ingredients in a small bowl. Cover and chill for at least 1 hour before using.

• MAKES ½ CUP.

•   •   •   •

CARL'S JR.
THE SIX DOLLAR BURGER

☆   ✌   💣   ✏   ☯   ✂   ☞

In 2001 this West Coast chain came up with a great idea: Clone the type of burger you'd get at a casual restaurant chain such as Chili's or T.G.I. Friday's for around six bucks, but sell it for just $3.95. It's ⅓ pound of ground beef stacked on top of plenty of fixings, including red onion and those sweet-tasting bread-and-butter pickle slices. And the cost of a Six Dollar Burger gets even lower when you make your own version at home: How does less than two bucks grab ya?

⅓ pound ground beef
salt
pepper
1 large sesame seed bun
3 teaspoons mayonnaise
1 teaspoon mustard
2 teaspoons ketchup

2 slices American cheese
3 or 4 bread-and-butter pickle
  slices
leaf of iceberg lettuce
2 large tomato slices
4 or 5 red onion rings

1. Preheat a barbecue or indoor grill to medium heat.
2. Form the ground beef into a patty with a slightly larger diameter than the sesame seed bun.
3. Grill the burger for 3 to 4 minutes per side, or until done. Be sure to lightly salt and pepper each side of the patty.
4. While the patty grills, brown the faces of the bun in a hot skillet over medium heat.
5. After the buns have browned, spread about 1½ teaspoons of mayonnaise on the face of the top bun half, as well as on the bottom bun half.

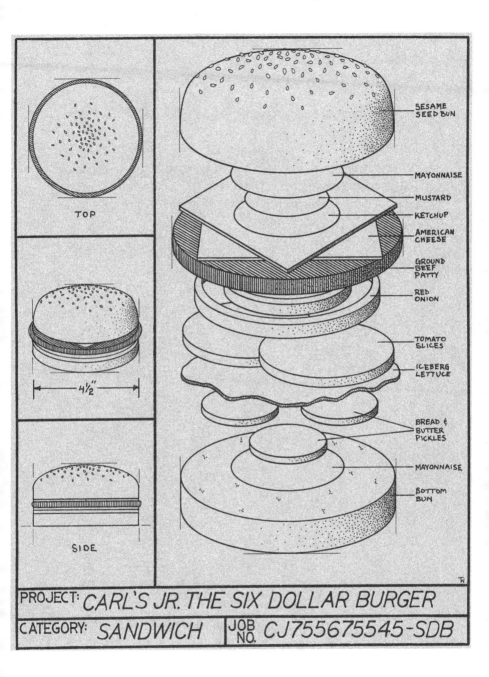

TOP

4½"

SIDE

SESAME SEED BUN
MAYONNAISE
MUSTARD
KETCHUP
AMERICAN CHEESE
GROUND BEEF PATTY
RED ONION
TOMATO SLICES
ICEBERG LETTUCE
BREAD & BUTTER PICKLES
MAYONNAISE
BOTTOM BUN

PROJECT: *CARL'S JR. THE SIX DOLLAR BURGER*

CATEGORY: *SANDWICH*   **JOB NO.** *CJ755675545-SDB*

6. Spread 1 teaspoon of mustard on the face of the top bun half, followed by 2 teaspoons of ketchup.
7. Arrange 3 or 4 bread-and-butter pickle slices on the bottom bun half.
8. Arrange the lettuce leaf on the pickles, followed by the tomato slices and red onion.
9. When the beef is cooked, arrange 2 slices of American cheese on the patty, let it melt a bit, then place the top bun half on the cheese and scoop up the whole thing with a spatula and place it on the bottom half of the burger.

• MAKES 1 HAMBURGER.

• • • •

CARNEGIE DELI CLASSIC NEW YORK CITY CHEESECAKE

☆   ✌   💣   ✐   🎱   ✂   ☞

Carnegie Deli's huge pastrami sandwiches were selected as the best in New York by *New York Magazine* in 1975, but it's the cheesecakes, which can be shipped anywhere in the country, that really put this famous deli on the map. The secret to accurately cloning a traditional New York cheesecake is in creating the perfect not-too-sweet sugar cookie crust and varying the baking temperature so that you get a nicely browned top before cooking the cheesecake through. Get ready for the best deli-style cheesecake to ever come out of your oven.

COOKIE CRUST
½ cup (1 stick) butter, softened
¼ cup granulated sugar
½ teaspoon vanilla extract
pinch salt
1 egg
1 ½ cups all-purpose flour

FILLING
five 8-ounce packages cream
   cheese, softened
1 ⅓ cups granulated sugar
2 teaspoons vanilla extract
4 teaspoons lemon juice
⅓ cup sour cream
2 tablespoons all-purpose flour
3 eggs

1. Leave the butter and cream cheese out of the refrigerator for 30 to 60 minutes to soften. Make the crust by creaming together the butter, sugar, vanilla, and salt. Add the egg and mix well. Add the flour and stir well to combine.
2. Preheat the oven to 375 degrees F, then press half of the dough

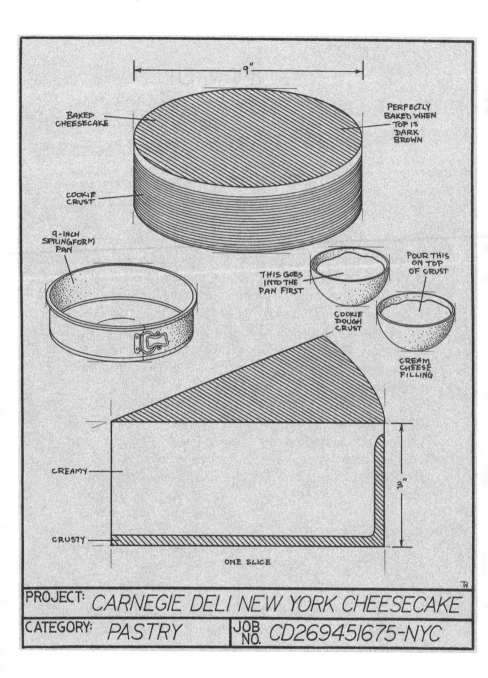

9"

BAKED
CHEESECAKE

PERFECTLY
BAKED WHEN
TOP IS
DARK
BROWN

COOKIE
CRUST

9-INCH
SPRINGFORM
PAN

THIS GOES
INTO THE
PAN FIRST

POUR THIS
ON TOP
OF CRUST

COOKIE
DOUGH
CRUST

CREAM
CHEESE
FILLING

CREAMY

3"

CRUSTY

ONE SLICE

TW

PROJECT: *CARNEGIE DELI NEW YORK CHEESECAKE*

CATEGORY: *PASTRY*   JOB NO. *CD269451675-NYC*

onto the bottom of a 9-inch springform pan. Bake for 5 to 7 minutes, or until the edge of the dough begins to turn light brown. Cool.

3. Take the remaining dough and press it around the inside edge of the pan. Don't go all the way up to the top though. Leave about a ½-inch margin from the top of the pan.

4. Crank oven up to 500 degrees F. To make the filling, combine the cream cheese, sugar, vanilla, and lemon juice with an electric mixer in a large bowl until smooth. Mix in the sour cream and flour. Add the eggs and mix on low speed until combined.

5. Pour the cream cheese filling into the pan and bake for 10 minutes. Reduce the heat to 350 degrees F and bake for 30 to 35 minutes more, or until the center is firm. Cool completely, then cover and chill in refrigerator for several hours or overnight before serving.

• SERVES 8.

• • • •

CHEX MIX
BOLD PARTY BLEND

☆ ✌ 💣 ✏ ☯ ✂ ☞

Little checkerboard squares of rice, corn, and wheat are worth big bucks! In 1996 General Mills paid $570 million to Ralston Purina for the entire brand of Chex cereals and snack mixes. As it turns out, developing these cereals into a convenient snack mix brand was a very smart move. When I was a kid the only way to get Chex Mix was to make it myself from a recipe on the box of Chex Cereal. Today Chex Mix comes in nearly a dozen different flavors, including chocolate, cheddar, honey nut, and hot & spicy. But a home version using the recipe on the cereal box never tastes the same as the stuff in the bags. That's because the recipe leaves out a very important secret ingredient: MSG, or monosodium glutamate. This amino acid salt enhances the other flavors in the bag and gives the snack mix its addictive taste. You can find MSG in grocery stores near the salt (Accent Flavor Enhancer is one popular brand name). Add a little of that to your creative mix of Chex Cereal, pretzels, crackers, and breadsticks, along with some white cheddar popcorn seasoning, soy sauce, Worcestershire sauce, and a few other common ingredients, and you'll have easily cloned one of the most popular Chex Mix flavors.

½ tablespoon margarine
1 ½ tablespoons vegetable oil
2 teaspoons Worcestershire sauce
¼ teaspoon soy sauce
1 ¼ teaspoons white cheddar popcorn seasoning

1 teaspoon monosodium glutamate (such as Accent Flavor Enhancer)
¼ teaspoon garlic powder
¼ teaspoon onion powder

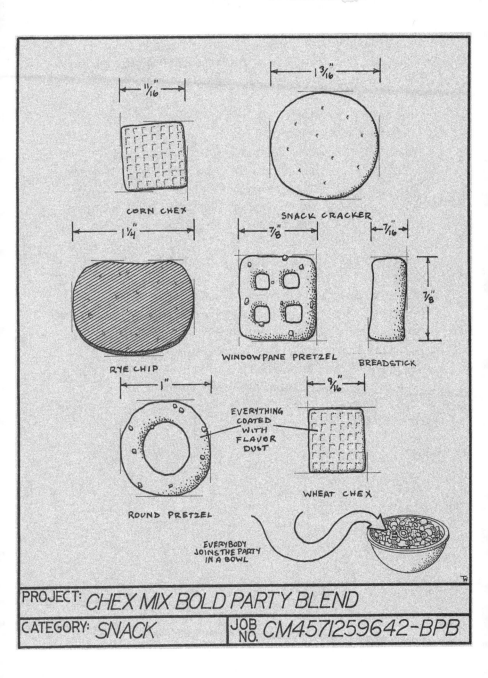

CORN CHEX

SNACK CRACKER

RYE CHIP

WINDOWPANE PRETZEL

BREADSTICK

EVERYTHING COATED WITH FLAVOR DUST

WHEAT CHEX

ROUND PRETZEL

EVERYBODY JOINS THE PARTY IN A BOWL

PROJECT: *CHEX MIX BOLD PARTY BLEND*

CATEGORY: *SNACK*

JOB NO. *CM4571259642-BPB*

*6 cups of a blend of Corn Chex,
Wheat Chex, pretzels, mini
crackers, cheese-flavored*

*crackers, thin breadsticks
(broken into bite-size bits), or
whatever you like*

1. Preheat the oven to 325 degrees F.
2. Melt the margarine in a small bowl in your microwave oven and whisk with the oil, Worcestershire sauce, and soy sauce.
3. Combine the white cheddar popcorn seasoning, MSG, garlic powder, and onion powder in a small bowl.
4. Pour your blend of Chex, crackers, and pretzels into a large zip-top plastic bag. Whisk the margarine and oil mixture again and pour about a quarter into the bag. Seal the bag and shake. Repeat with the remaining margarine and oil mixture until the dry stuff is well coated.
5. Pour the mix out of the bag onto a large baking sheet and bake for 6 minutes, or until the mix is crispy but not brown. Stir the mix around halfway through baking.
6. Cool the mix for a couple of minutes, and then pour it into another zip-top bag. Spoon about a quarter of the white cheddar popcorn seasoning mixture into the bag, seal it, and give it a good shake. Repeat this process until all of the seasoning is gone. Pour the contents of the bag into a serving bowl and munch out.

• MAKES 6 CUPS.

•   •   •   •

CHICK-FIL-A
HONEY ROASTED BBQ SAUCE

☆　　　✌　　　💣　　　✏　　　☯　　　✂　　　☞

It's sweet, it's tangy, it's smoky, it's delicious; and it's available only in blister packs by request at one of the 1,237 U.S. Chick-fil-A locations that dot the country. I guess that's why so many of you asked for a clone—those blister packs are small! But alas, with this Top Secret formula, you'll have a heaping one cup of a taste-alike version of the delicious sauce to use as you wish; be it as a spread on your favorite sandwiches or as a dressing on a grilled chicken salad.

$1/2$ cup vegetable oil
$1/4$ cup honey
1 tablespoon Grey Poupon Dijon
　mustard
1 teaspoon ketchup
1 teaspoon granulated sugar
$1/4$ teaspoon paprika
$1/4$ teaspoon salt
$1/8$ teaspoon ground black pepper

$1/8$ teaspoon garlic powder
$1/8$ teaspoon onion powder
$2 1/2$ tablespoons white vinegar
$1/2$ teaspoon concentrated hickory
　liquid smoke flavoring
$1/4$ teaspoon lemon juice
1 egg yolk
1 teaspoon water

1. Combine the oil, honey, mustard, ketchup, sugar, paprika, salt, pepper, garlic powder, and onion powder in a small saucepan. Place over medium heat, and then heat until boiling. Stir. Remove the pan from the heat and let it cool uncovered for 10 minutes. Add the vinegar, smoke flavoring, and lemon juice.

2. While the sauce cools, vigorously whisk the egg yolk with 1 teaspoon water in a medium bowl for about 2 minutes, or until the color is pale yellow.

3. Drizzle the cooled sauce mixture into the egg yolk mixture in a steady stream while rapidly whisking. This will create a thick, creamy emulsion that will prevent the oil from separating. Cover the sauce and chill it until it's needed.

• MAKES ABOUT 1 CUP.

Tidbits

The vinegar kills any potentially harmful bacteria from the raw egg. If you are concerned, use a pasteurized egg product as a substitute.

•   •   •   •

CHICK-FIL-A
CARROT AND RAISIN SALAD

☆   ✌   💣   ✏   🎱   ✂   ☞

The secret to cloning this chicken chain's popular carrot raisin salad lies in proper carrot shredding technique. A standard shredder, like the type you might use to shred a hunk of cheddar cheese, creates a coarse shred that makes the salad taste much too "carroty." Instead, find yourself the type of fine shredder that is often used for Parmesan cheese. Sure, it'll take a little more elbow grease to reduce 5 or 6 carrots to ultra thin strips, but I guarantee you'll end up with a superior finished product that will help you forget all about the extra effort.

$1/3$ cup mayonnaise
2 teaspoons lemon juice
2 tablespoons granulated sugar
2 tablespoons canned crushed
  pineapple

4 cups finely shredded carrots
  (5 to 6 carrots)
$1/3$ cup raisins

1. Whisk together the mayonnaise, lemon juice, and sugar in a large bowl until the sugar is mostly dissolved.
2. Whisk in the crushed pineapple.
3. Fold in the shredded carrots and raisins. Cover and chill overnight before serving.

• MAKES 8 SMALL SERVINGS.

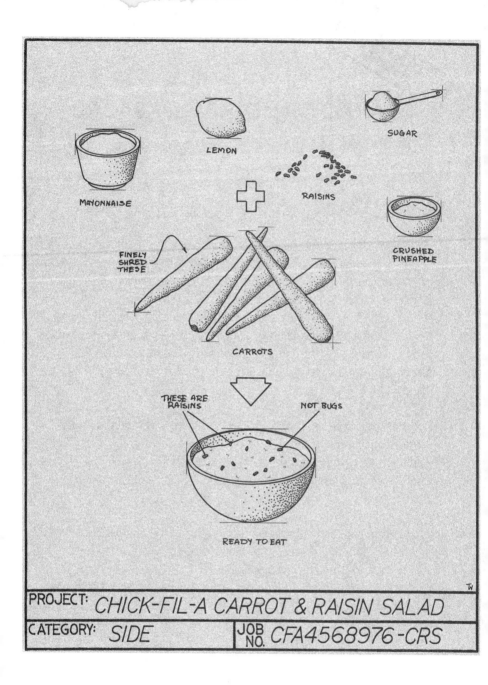

MAYONNAISE

LEMON

SUGAR

RAISINS

FINELY SHRED THESE

CRUSHED PINEAPPLE

CARROTS

THESE ARE RAISINS

NOT BUGS

READY TO EAT

PROJECT:	*CHICK-FIL-A CARROT & RAISIN SALAD*	
CATEGORY: *SIDE*	JOB NO.	*CFA4568976-CRS*

CHIPOTLE MEXICAN GRILL CHIPOTLE-HONEY VINAIGRETTE

☆　　✌　　💣　　✏　　👁　　✂　　☞

Steve Ells used his Culinary Institute of America training to develop a simple menu for the first Chipotle Mexican Grill he opened in 1993 near the University of Denver. Today Chipotle has grown to more than 700 units, and the chain continues to serve a relatively limited selection (compared to other Mexican chains) of burritos, tacos, and salads that are made to order, with unprocessed and hormone-free ingredients. Just as when ordering a burrito or taco, you get to choose the meat, beans, salsa, and cheese that will top your romaine lettuce salad. The finishing touch is an amazing house dressing that's made fresh every day. It's sweet, it's tangy, it's smoky, and it's packing some heat. It's also a quick recipe to duplicate with just a blender and a dozen common ingredients, including ground chipotle chile, which you can usually find near the ground cayenne. After you whip up this dressing, let it chill out in the fridge for an hour or two. This recipe will give you enough dressing for at least 10 salads.

$^1/_2$ cup red wine vinegar
$^1/_3$ cup honey
2 teaspoons Grey Poupon Dijon mustard
1 $^1/_4$ teaspoons ground chipotle chile
1 teaspoon lime juice

$^3/_4$ teaspoon ground black pepper
$^3/_4$ teaspoon salt
$^1/_2$ teaspoon paprika
$^1/_4$ teaspoon garlic powder
$^1/_4$ teaspoon onion powder
$^1/_4$ teaspoon dried oregano
$^1/_2$ cup extra virgin olive oil

1. Combine all the ingredients except the oil in a blender and blend on low speed for 10 seconds.

2. Slowly drizzle the olive oil into the blender through the hole in the lid while blending on low speed. When all the oil is added, pour the dressing into a container, cover, and chill for an hour or more.

- MAKES 1½ CUPS.

• • • •

CHIPOTLE MEXICAN GRILL BARBACOA BURRITO

☆　✌　💣　✒　◉　✂　☞

The original Mexican barbacoa was traditionally prepared by cooking almost any kind of meat—goat, fish, chicken, or cow cheek meat, to name just a few—in a pit covered with leaves over low heat for many hours, until tender. When the dish made its way into the United States via Texas the word transformed into "barbecue" and the preparation changed to incorporate aboveground techniques such as smoking and grilling. The good news is that we can re-create the beef barbacoa that Chipotle has made popular on its ginormous burritos without digging any holes in our yard or tracking down a local source for fresh cow faces. After braising about 30 pounds of chuck roasts, I finally discovered the perfect clone with a taste-alike adobo sauce that fills your roast with flavor as it slowly cooks to a fork-tender delicacy on your stovetop over 5 to 6 hours. Part of the secret for great adobo sauce is toasting whole cumin seeds and cloves and then grinding them up in a coffee grinder (measure the spices after grinding them). Since the braising process takes so long, start early in the day and get ready for a big dinner, because I've also included clones here for Chipotle's pico de gallo, pinto beans, and delicious cilantro-lime rice to make your burritos complete. You can add your choice of cheese, plus guacamole and sour cream for a super-deluxe clone version.

BARBACOA

⅓ cup apple cider vinegar
3 tablespoons lime juice

3 to 4 canned chipotle chiles
4 garlic cloves

4 teaspoons freshly toasted and
ground cumin seeds (see
Tidbits)
2 teaspoons dried Mexican
oregano
1 1/2 teaspoons ground black
pepper
1 1/2 teaspoons salt

1/2 teaspoon freshly toasted
and ground cloves (see
Tidbits)
2 tablespoons vegetable oil
4 to 5 pound chuck roast
3/4 cup chicken broth
3 bay leaves

PICO DE GALLO

4 medium tomatoes, diced
1/2 cup diced red onion
1/4 cup minced fresh cilantro
2 tablespoons minced jalapeño
pepper

2 tablespoons lime juice
1/4 teaspoon salt

PINTO BEANS

three 15-ounce cans pinto beans
(with liquid)
3 tablespoons bacon fat (from
cooking 3 to 4 pieces of bacon)

1/2 teaspoon dried Mexican
oregano

CILANTRO-LIME RICE

3 cups water
2 cups converted rice
3 tablespoons butter

1 1/2 teaspoons salt
1/3 cup minced fresh cilantro
2 tablespoons lime juice

FOR THE BURRITOS

eight 12-inch flour tortillas
shredded cheddar cheese or
Monterey Jack cheese

guacamole (optional)
sour cream (optional)

1. Make the adobo sauce by combining the vinegar, lime juice,
   chipotles, garlic, cumin, oregano, black pepper, salt, and cloves in
   a blender or food processor and puree on high speed until
   smooth.

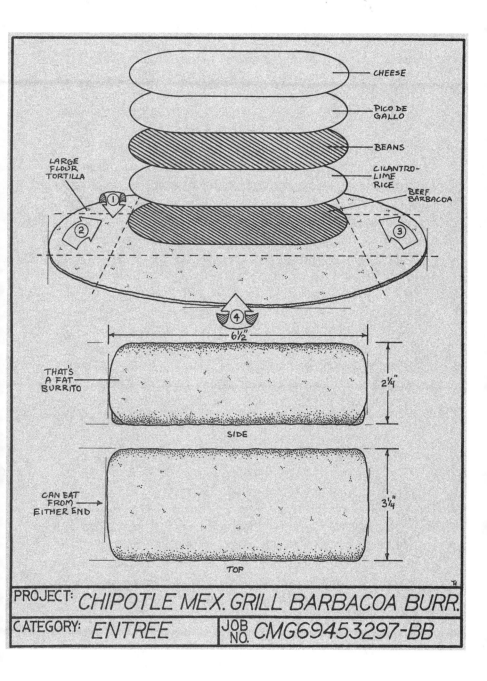

CHEESE

PICO DE GALLO

BEANS

LARGE FLOUR TORTILLA

CILANTRO-LIME RICE

BEEF BARBACOA

① ② ③ ④

THAT'S A FAT BURRITO

6½"

2¼"

SIDE

CAN EAT FROM → EITHER END

3¼"

TOP

PROJECT: *CHIPOTLE MEX. GRILL BARBACOA BURR.*

CATEGORY: *ENTREE*   **JOB NO.** *CMG69453297-BB*

2. Trim the fat from the meat, then slice the roast into 6 smaller pieces. Sear all sides of the chunks of meat in the oil in a large stockpot or Dutch oven over medium heat until browned. Add the adobo sauce to the meat, pour in the chicken broth, and add the bay leaves. Cover the pot, turn your stove to medium-low heat, and let the meat simmer (braise) for 5 to 6 hours, or until the meat easily flakes apart. Turn the meat every 30 minutes as it cooks. After 4 hours, keep the lid off the pot. At the 5-hour mark, you should be able to tear the meat apart into bite-size chunks with tongs.

3. As soon as your meat is in the pot, make the pico de gallo by combining all the ingredients in a bowl. Cover and chill for several hours while the barbacoa is cooking.

4. Just before the meat is done, prepare the pinto beans by combining the beans with the bacon fat and oregano in a medium saucepan. Simmer for 30 to 40 minutes, or until most of the liquid is gone and beans are soft. Keep the beans covered until the meat is ready.

5. Make the cilantro-lime rice by combining the water, rice, butter, and salt in a large saucepan. Bring to a boil over medium heat, then reduce the heat to low, cover the saucepan, and simmer for 20 minutes. When the rice is done, stir in the cilantro and lime juice. Keep the rice covered until you're ready to assemble the burritos.

6. Make each burrito by first heating a flour tortilla on a large skillet over medium heat or wrapped in moist paper towels in the microwave. When the tortilla is warm, spoon a healthy portion of barbacoa meat into the tortilla, followed by the cilantro-lime rice, beans, pico de gallo, and your choice of cheese. You can also add sour cream and/or guacamole if you like. Fold the bottom edge of the tortilla over the filling, then fold in the ends. Continue rolling the burrito up and away from you until it's rolled up tight, and dig in.

- MAKES 8 LARGE BURRITOS.

Tidbits

Toast whole cumin seeds and cloves separately in a small sauté pan over medium-low heat. Toss often and watch the spices closely so they don't burn. The spices are done toasting when they are fragrant and slightly browned. Use a clean coffee grinder to grind each of the spices to a powder, and then measure for the recipe.

•　•　•　•

CLIFF & BUSTER
COCONUT MACAROONS

☆　　♨　　💣　　✏　　☯　　✂　　☞

While passing these out to each giddy audience member on her 2003 "Favorite Things" show, Oprah gushed, "Isn't that the best macaroon you've ever had?" The recipe for these delicious yet easy-to-clone coconut macaroons was passed down to Cliff Barsevich years ago from his grandmother, and they were served at the events serviced by Cliff and partner Ron Strle's catering business. When customers continued to rave about the cookies, the duo began selling the macaroons by the box in high-end stores such as Neiman Marcus. With a lot of help from *The Oprah Winfrey Show*, the cookies have become a huge success. Still, at 15 bucks a dozen, it's nice to have a clone that will satisfy your macaroon munchies at a fraction of the cost. It's the closest we'll ever get to a homemade version since Cliff says he's never sharing the recipe. He says when he dies he's taking the secret formula with him.

MACAROONS

3 cups unsweetened shredded coconut (about 8 ounces—see Tidbits)

⅓ cup sweetened condensed milk

¾ teaspoon vanilla extract

¾ teaspoon almond extract

pinch salt

CHOCOLATE GANACHE

½ cup semisweet chocolate chips

3 tablespoons heavy cream

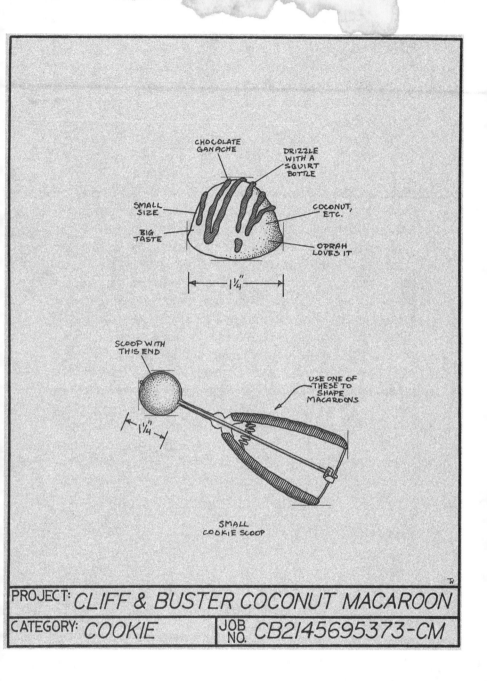

CHOCOLATE
GANACHE

DRIZZLE
WITH A
SQUIRT
BOTTLE

SMALL
SIZE

COCONUT,
ETC.

BIG
TASTE

OPRAH
LOVES IT

1¼"

SCOOP WITH
THIS END

USE ONE OF
THESE TO
SHAPE
MACAROONS

1¼"

SMALL
COOKIE SCOOP

PROJECT: CLIFF & BUSTER COCONUT MACAROON

CATEGORY: COOKIE

JOB NO. CB2145695373-CM

1. Preheat the oven to 350 degrees F.
2. Dump the shredded coconut into a large bowl.
3. Stir the vanilla, almond extract, and salt into the condensed milk.
4. Drizzle the condensed milk over the coconut while tossing the coconut to coat it thoroughly.
5. When the coconut and condensed milk are combined, use a 1¼-inch cookie scoop to mold the macaroons. Press the macaroon mixture firmly into the scoop, then turn it out onto a sheet pan. Bake the macaroons for 12 to 15 minutes, or until you see the top of the macaroons beginning to turn light brown. Remove the macaroons from the oven and let them cool.
6. As the macaroons cool, resist the temptation to eat them. Instead, prepare the chocolate ganache by combining the chocolate chips with the cream in a small glass or ceramic cup or bowl. Microwave this on 50 percent power for 1 minute, then gently stir the chocolate. If the chocolate is not completely melted after a couple minutes of stirring, microwave it again for another 30 seconds on half power and stir. Be careful not to overcook the chips or the chocolate will seize up and your ganache will be grainy instead of smooth. If that happens, start over. Sorry. Now you can have a macaroon.
7. When the chocolate is melted and smooth, pour it into a squirt bottle and drizzle it in thin streams over each macaroon. Let the macaroons sit out for a few hours. At a room temperature of 72 degrees the chocolate should set in 3 or 4 hours. When the chocolate has set, store the macaroons in an airtight container for up to 14 days at room temperature or for up to 4 weeks in the fridge.

• MAKES 20 MACAROONS.

Tidbits

The real Cliff & Buster's macaroons use a thinly shredded short flake unsweetened coconut, which can be found in specialty stores such as Trader Joe's. If you can't track down this type of coconut, using the more common sweetened stuff found in just about every supermarket will make a slightly sweeter, yet still delicious cookie.

COCA-COLA BLĀK

Two years is all it took for Coca-Cola to banish this new hybrid of cola and black coffee to the land of the Dead Foods in 2008. It may have been the steep price that scared customers away, since they were now getting a smaller-size (8 ounces) Coca-Cola beverage for $1.79. Others claim it was the unusual flavor, although I actually thought it tasted pretty good—like a combination of Coca-Cola, cream soda, and coffee. Hey now, that sounds like a pretty good place to start with our clone recipe. Simply dissolve some Nutra-Sweet (that's what Coca-Cola uses) in cold espresso, add it to the sodas, and you'll get 24 ounces (3 servings) of a remarkable clone at a total cost of just 90 cents. That's more like it! Another Dead Food resurrected.

2 tablespoons cold espresso
  (or strong coffee)
¼ teaspoon NutraSweet
  (1 packet)

one 12-ounce can Coca-Cola
one 12-ounce can A & W Cream
  Soda

1. Dissolve the NutraSweet in the espresso.
2. Combine the espresso, Coca-Cola, and cream soda and serve 1 cup (8 ounces) over ice.

• MAKES 3 SERVINGS.

Tidbits

My math above is based on the price of cans of cola and cream soda when purchased in 12-packs.

• • • •

CRUNCH 'N MUNCH
BUTTERY TOFFEE POPCORN
WITH PEANUTS

☆   ✌   💣   ✏   ☯   ✂   ☞

Just look at what F. W. Rueckheim started. He was the guy who, back in the late 1800s, made candy-coated popcorn a national treasure with the invention of Cracker Jack. Now we've got Fiddle Faddle, Screaming Yellow Zonkers, Crunch 'n Munch, and several brands of candy-coated microwave popcorn, to name just a few. Sure, these other varieties don't have the traditional prize inside the box, but let's face it, those prizes are pretty weak compared to what used to be found at the bottom of a box of Cracker Jack when I was a kid. And the old-fashioned molasses formula used on Cracker Jack just doesn't have the pizzazz of some of the other tantalizing flavors coating popcorn today. The butter toffee coating is a good example, so that's what I've reverse-engineered for you here. It's a simple recipe that makes a finished product so addictive you'll have to beg someone to take it away from you before you finish the whole bowl by yourself. All you need is a candy thermometer, some microwave popcorn, and a few other basic ingredients and you're about 15 minutes away from candy-coated popcorn heaven.

8 cups popped microwave popcorn (natural flavor)	¹/₂ cup (1 stick) butter
¹/₄ cup Spanish peanuts	¹/₂ cup granulated sugar
	¹/₄ cup light corn syrup

1. Spread the popcorn and peanuts on a baking sheet and keep it warm in your oven set to 300 degrees F while you prepare the butter toffee. You don't need to preheat the oven.

2. Melt the butter in a medium saucepan over medium-low heat.
3. Add the sugar and corn syrup and simmer, stirring occasionally. Pop a candy thermometer into the mixture and watch it closely.
4. When the thermometer reaches 300 degrees F, pour the candy over the warm popcorn and peanuts. Stir well so that the candy coats the popcorn. Put the popcorn back into the oven for 5 minutes, then stir it again to coat the popcorn. Repeat if necessary to thoroughly coat all the popcorn.
5. Pour the coated popcorn and peanuts onto wax paper. When cool, break up the chunks into bite-size pieces and store it all in a covered container.

- MAKES 8 CUPS.

• • • •

DAIRY QUEEN MOOLATTÉ

Here's what happens behind the counter when you order a Cappuccino MooLatté frozen coffee drink at Dairy Queen: A plastic cup is filled almost halfway with the frozen simple syrup mix that comes out of the machine used for slush drinks. Next, your server hops over to the frozen soft-serve machine and fills the cup the rest of the way with ice cream. After a couple squirts of concentrated coffee syrup, the drink is blended on a milkshake machine and is then passed off to you in exchange for a few greenbacks. Since we don't have the same cool commercial equipment they use over at Dairy Queen, we'll have to make our clone in a common household blender. First things first, we need to start with very strong coffee. Make some espresso, or pick some up at your nearest coffeehouse. After dissolving sugar in the coffee, chill it, and then add it to ice cream, ice, and milk in a blender, and get it going. When the blender blades come to a halt, you'll have two 16-ounce clones of the DQ frozen coffee drink fave ready for whipped cream. If you prefer the mocha or caramel variety of the MooLatté, jump to the bottom, where the Tidbits will throw those variations your way.

1 cup espresso
⅓ cup granulated sugar
3 cups ice

2 cups vanilla ice cream
¼ cup whole milk

GARNISH
canned whipped cream

1. Dissolve the sugar in the espresso, and then chill the espresso until cold.
2. Combine all the ingredients in a blender and blend on high speed until the ice is crushed and drink is smooth.
3. Pour into two 16-ounce glasses and serve with straws and whipped cream on top.

- MAKES TWO 16-OUNCE SERVINGS.

Tidbits

To duplicate the mocha version of the MooLatté, simply reduce the granulated sugar in the above recipe to ¼ cup, then add ¼ cup of fudge topping to the blender before blending.

For the caramel version, reduce the granulated sugar to ¼ cup, then add ¼ cup of caramel topping to the blender.

•   •   •   •

DEL TACO
CRISPY FISH TACO

☆　　✌　　💣　　✏　　☯　　✂　　☞

The number two Mexican fast-food chain nicely duplicates the delicious fish tacos you'd find in coastal towns south of the border: two corn tortillas wrapped around a fried halibut fillet that's topped with cabbage, fresh salsa, and a creamy "secret sauce." It's practically impossible to eat just one—they're that good. And, thanks to the availability of breaded frozen fish sticks in just about every market, a home clone is stupidly simple. If you can't find crispy halibut sticks in your local store, the more common breaded pollack will work just fine here. You can also use frozen fish portions that are grilled if you're not into the breaded (fried) stuff. The real recipe at Del Taco comes with two thin corn tortillas, but the corn tortillas found in consumer markets are usually thicker, so you may prefer just one tortilla per taco.

SECRET SAUCE
$1/4$ cup mayonnaise
1 tablespoon whole milk

$1/2$ teaspoon lime juice

SALSA
2 medium tomatoes, diced (about
　$1 1/2$ cups)
$1/2$ medium Spanish onion, diced
　(about $3/4$ cup)
2 tablespoons chopped fresh
　cilantro
1 teaspoon lime juice

$1/4$ teaspoon salt
$1/4$ teaspoon ground black pepper
$1/8$ teaspoon cayenne pepper
8 frozen fish sticks (halibut or
　pollack)
2 cups shredded cabbage
16 small corn tortillas

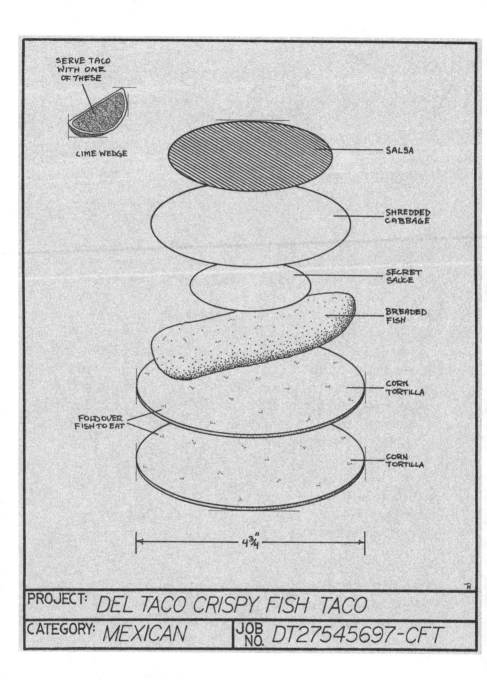

SERVE TACO
WITH ONE
OF THESE

LIME WEDGE

SALSA

SHREDDED
CABBAGE

SECRET
SAUCE

BREADED
FISH

CORN
TORTILLA

FOLD OVER
FISH TO EAT

CORN
TORTILLA

$4\frac{3}{4}''$

PROJECT: *DEL TACO CRISPY FISH TACO*

CATEGORY: *MEXICAN*   **JOB NO.** *DT27545697-CFT*

GARNISH
8 lime wedges

1. Make the secret sauce by combining the mayonnaise, milk, and lime juice in a small bowl. Whisk until smooth, and then cover and chill until needed.
2. Make the salsa by combining all the ingredients in a medium bowl. Cover and chill this as well until your fish is baked and you're ready to build the tacos.
3. Bake the frozen fish sticks as directed on the box.
4. Warm the tortillas in the microwave in a tortilla warmer, or wrap them in moist paper towels before nuking.
5. Build each taco using two tortillas per taco. Drop a fish stick into the center of the tortillas, and then spoon about 1½ teaspoons of sauce over the fish. Add about ¼ cup of cabbage and top off the taco with a couple dollops of salsa. Serve each taco with a lime wedge.

- MAKES 8 TACOS.

•　•　•　•

DUNCAN HINES
MOIST DELUXE YELLOW
CAKE MIX

☆   ✄   ●   ✎   ◑   ✂   ☞

So, you need to make some buttery yellow cake, but you don't have any mix in the pantry. Or perhaps you love the moist and delicious cake made from a box but aren't a big fan of all the polysyllabic preservatives and thickeners that come along for the ride. Well, here is the TSR way to make homemade yellow cake mix using basic baking ingredients. You can store the cloned dry mix in a sealed container for several weeks in a cabinet until you need it. Then, when you're ready to make the cake, simply add water, oil, and eggs to the mix in the exact measurements required by the original; pour the batter into a pan and pop it in the oven. Done.

3 cups cake flour
2 cups baker's sugar (superfine sugar)
2 teaspoons baking powder
2 teaspoon baking soda
1 1/4 teaspoons salt

1/2 cup shortening
2 teaspoons vanilla extract
2 teaspoons imitation butter flavoring (see Tidbits)
10 drops yellow food coloring

TO MAKE THE CAKE
1 1/3 cups water
1/3 cup vegetable oil

3 large eggs

1. Combine the flour, sugar, baking powder, baking soda, and salt in a large bowl. Stir to combine.

2. Combine the shortening, vanilla, butter flavoring, and food coloring with an electric mixer in a small bowl. Spoon the shortening mixture into the dry ingredients and beat well with the electric mixer on medium speed. Mix until no chunks of shortening are visible. The mixture should resemble cornmeal. This is your cake mix, which you can now keep in a sealed container for several weeks until you are ready to make the cake.

3. To make the cake, preheat the oven to 350 degrees F. Grease the sides and bottom of two 9-inch baking pans or one 13 x 9-inch pan. Lightly flour the greased pans.

4. Blend the dry cake mix (from step #1) with the water, oil, and eggs in a large bowl with an electric mixer at low speed until moistened. Increase the speed to medium and beat for 2 more minutes.

5. Pour the batter into the pans and bake for 30 to 33 minutes for 9-inch pans, and 35 to 38 minutes for a 13 x 9-inch pan. You can also make 2 dozen cupcakes with the mix. They take 19 to 22 minutes.

• MAKES TWO 9-INCH ROUND CAKES, OR ONE 13 x 9-INCH SHEET CAKE.

Tidbits

You'll find imitation butter flavoring near the vanilla extract in the baking aisle of your favorite food store.

•   •   •   •

DUNKIN' DONUTS
COFFEE COOLATTA

☆　　✌　　●　　✏　　☉　　✄　　☞

All it takes is one slurp of Dunkin' Donuts' hit frozen coffee drink to determine there is much more than concentrated coffee, sugar, and milk in there. I detect vanilla and hazelnut flavors, but adding just a bit of almond extract and some chocolate syrup completes the flavor profile. Torani makes hazelnut syrup that's perfect for this recipe— you'll find it near the coffee in your market or in a bar supply outlet. Your drink will come out lighter in color than the real thing, since the chain apparently uses caramel coloring to darken the formula. This recipe makes one 24-ounce serving—that's called "medium" at the store—or you can split it into two more modest 12-ounce servings.

1 1/4 cups strong coffee, cold (see step #1)
1 cup milk
5 tablespoons granulated sugar
2 tablespoons Hershey's chocolate syrup

1 tablespoon Torani hazelnut syrup
1 teaspoon vanilla extract
1/4 teaspoon almond extract
2 1/2 cups ice cubes

1. Brew strong coffee by using twice the amount of grounds required by your coffeemaker. Chill the coffee in your refrigerator until it's cold.
2. Combine the cold coffee, milk, sugar, chocolate syrup, hazelnut syrup, vanilla, and almond extract in a blender and blend for 1 minute on low to dissolve sugar.

3. Add the ice and blend on high until ice is crushed and drink is smooth. Pour into a tall 24-ounce glass or two 12-ounce glasses, and serve with straws.

- MAKES ONE 24-OUNCE SERVING OR TWO 12-OUNCE SERVINGS.

• • • •

EINSTEIN BROS. BAGELS SANTA FE EGG SANDWICH

☆ ✌ 💣 ✎ ☯ ✄ ☞

If your crew likes food with a little kick and they're into breakfast sandwiches, grab some of your favorite bagels and give this clone a go. The jalapeño salsa cream cheese used here is made with only four ingredients, and the rest of the recipe is even easier: Cook up some turkey sausage patties in a skillet and prepare each serving of scrambled eggs in a small bowl in the microwave so they fit perfectly on the bagels. For the turkey sausage, I used Wampler brand, which comes in 1-pound tubes, but you can also use small turkey breakfast links—just squeeze the sausage out of the casings and form your patties (ditch the casings). You can also use pork sausage if you like.

JALAPEÑO SALSA CREAM CHEESE

8 ounces cream cheese
¼ cup Ortega medium salsa
2 tablespoons minced canned
    jalapeño slices

⅛ teaspoon chili powder

SANDWICH

6 ounces turkey breakfast
    sausage
3 large eggs, beaten (about ⅔ cup)
2 bagels, sliced in half and lightly
    toasted

2 slices Pepper Jack singles
2 tablespoons Ortega medium
    salsa

1. First make your jalapeño salsa cream cheese by mixing all the ingredients together in a small bowl. Cover and chill until it's needed.
2. Make the turkey sausage patties by forming the sausage into two 3-ounce patties that are about 4½ inches in diameter. If you have time, form the patties on wax paper and freeze them to make handling easier. They will shrink when cooking to just the right size.
3. Beat the eggs in a bowl, then measure half (about ⅓ cup) into a bowl with approximately the same diameter as the bagels. Microwave each bowl (separately) for 1 to 1½ minutes on high, or until the egg is completely cooked.
4. Lightly toast all the bagel halves.
5. Spread about 2 teaspoons of the jalapeño salsa cream cheese on the toasted face of the bottom half of each bagel.
6. When the eggs are cooked, arrange them on the cream cheese on each bottom bagel half.
7. Lay a slice of Pepper Jack cheese on each of the egg layers.
8. Arrange a sausage patty on top of the cheese on each sandwich.
9. Spread about 2 teaspoons of salsa on the toasted face of each of the top bagel halves.
10. Top off the sandwiches with the top bagel halves, slice each sandwich in half, and serve while hot.

- MAKES 2 SANDWICHES.

•   •   •   •

EL POLLO LOCO
AVOCADO SALSA

This creamy green sauce is available at the salsa bar at each of the 389 El Pollo Loco outlets located throughout the western United States, and folks are going crazy over it. The problem is, you can only get it in small quantities at the restaurant, and once you taste a little there you're going to want a lot more of it at home. Use a food processor to mix this one up (everything but the cilantro and onion goes in there) and prepare for a delicious, spicy concoction that you can pour over your favorite homemade Mexican-style dishes, from taco salads to fajitas. Big props go out to Pancho Ochoa, who opened his first roadside chicken stand in Guasave, Mexico, in 1975. Today Pancho's El Pollo Loco is the number one quick-service, flame-broiled chicken chain in America.

1 ripe avocado	¾ teaspoon salt
1 jalapeño pepper, stemmed and quartered	2 tablespoons minced fresh cilantro
1 cup water	2 tablespoons diced onion
1 tablespoon white vinegar	

1. Combine the avocado, jalapeño, water, vinegar, and salt in a food processor. Puree the mixture for several seconds on high speed, or until the jalapeño is finely minced.
2. Pour the mixture into a medium bowl. Stir in the cilantro and onion. Cover and chill the salsa until you're ready to serve it.

- Makes 1½ cups.

EL POLLO LOCO
BBQ BLACK BEANS

☆ ✌ 💣 ✏ ⚫ ✂ ☞

If you dig the taste of traditional BBQ beans, you've got to love El Pollo Loco's sweet and spicy variation using black beans. The light smokiness in this clone comes from bacon fat, and cayenne pepper and green chiles give the beans a Southwestern flavor that's perfect on burritos or as a delicious side. The prep is a breeze since you conveniently combine two 15-ounce cans of black beans with the other secret ingredients in a saucepan and just let it simmer for an hour or so. When the beans are soft and the mixture is thick, commence with the scarfing.

Two 15-ounce cans black beans
   (with liquid)
1 1/2 cups water
1 cup chicken broth
1/2 cup dark brown sugar
3 tablespoons ketchup

3 tablespoons bacon fat (from
   2 to 3 pieces cooked bacon)
2 tablespoons red wine vinegar
2 tablespoons minced canned
   green chiles
1/4 teaspoon cayenne pepper

1. Combine all the ingredients in a medium saucepan and place over medium heat.
2. When the mixture begins to bubble, reduce the heat and simmer uncovered for 60 to 75 minutes, or until the beans are soft and the mixture thickens.

• MAKES 3 CUPS.

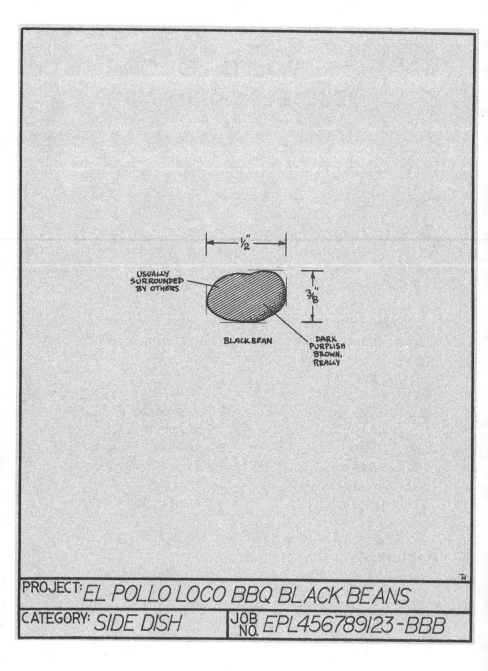

USUALLY SURROUNDED BY OTHERS

½"

⅜"

BLACK BEAN

DARK PURPLISH BROWN, REALLY

TW

PROJECT: *EL POLLO LOCO BBQ BLACK BEANS*

CATEGORY: *SIDE DISH* JOB NO. *EPL456789123-BBB*

EL POLLO LOCO
CREAMY CILANTRO DRESSING

☆　✌　💣　✏　☻　✂　☞

Sliced chicken breast, romaine lettuce, pico de gallo, tortilla strips, and cotija cheese make up El Pollo Loco's Caesar Salad, but it is the fantastic creamy cilantro dressing that gets the raves. Simply combine these basic ingredients in a bowl and you'll soon have more than 1 cup of the delicious dressing cloned and ready to pour over any of your home salad creations.

1 cup mayonnaise
1/3 cup whole milk
4 teaspoons finely minced fresh cilantro
2 teaspoons lime juice
1 teaspoon white vinegar
1 teaspoon granulated sugar

1 teaspoon finely minced garlic
1 teaspoon finely minced onion
1/2 teaspoon salt
1/8 teaspoon cayenne pepper
1/8 teaspoon ground black pepper
1/8 teaspoon ground cumin

Whisk together all the ingredients in a medium bowl. Cover and chill until you're ready to serve it.

• MAKES 1 1/4 CUPS.

FAMOUS AMOS
CHOCOLATE CHIP COOKIES

☆ ✌ 💣 ✏ 👁 ✂ ☞

Before Wally Amos shared his soon-to-be-famous homemade chocolate chip cookies with the world, he landed a job in the mail-room at the William Morris talent agency and soon became the agency's first African American talent agent. Wally's unique approach of sending performers boxes of homemade chocolate chip cookies that he developed from his aunt's secret recipe eventually helped him get Diana Ross and the Supremes as clients. After perfecting his cookie recipe in 1975, Wally launched his own cookie company and, solely from word of mouth, his baking business boomed. Today there are several flavors of Famous Amos Cookies, including oatmeal chocolate chip, oatmeal raisin, and peanut butter, but it is the plain chocolate chip cookies that are the most popular. The clone here will give you 100 little chocolate chip cookies just like the originals that are crunchy and small enough to dunk into a cold glass of moo juice.

1/2 cup shortening	1/4 cup milk
1/4 cup (1/2 stick) butter, softened	2 cups all-purpose flour
1/2 cup dark brown sugar	3/4 teaspoon baking soda
1/2 cup granulated sugar	1 teaspoon salt
1 egg	1 1/4 cups mini semisweet
1 teaspoon vanilla extract	chocolate chips

1. Preheat the oven to 325 degrees F.
2. Cream together shortening, butter, sugars, egg, and vanilla in a medium bowl with an electric mixer on medium speed until smooth. Mix in the milk.

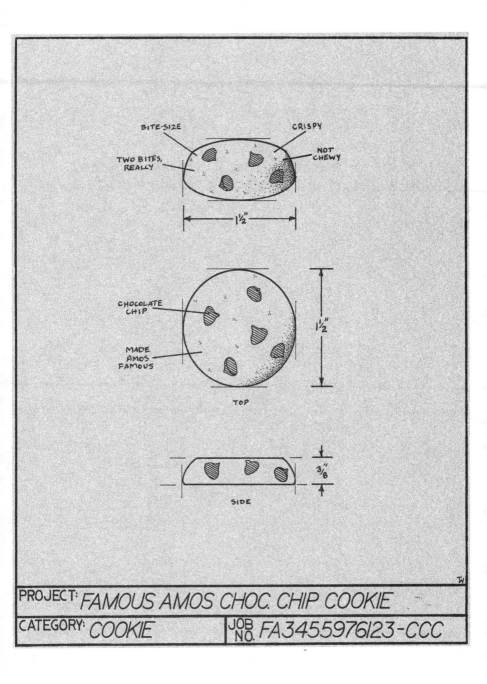

BITE-SIZE

CRISPY

TWO BITES, REALLY

NOT CHEWY

1½"

CHOCOLATE CHIP

1½"

MADE AMOS FAMOUS

TOP

3/8"

SIDE

PROJECT: *FAMOUS AMOS CHOC. CHIP COOKIE*

CATEGORY: *COOKIE*

JOB NO. *FA3455976123-CCC*

3. In a separate medium bowl, combine the flour, baking soda, and salt. Mix the dry ingredients into the wet ingredients, and then add the chocolate chips.
4. Measure 1 teaspoon of dough and roll it into a ball with your hands. Press the ball onto a parchment paper–lined baking sheet until it is about half the thickness it was as a ball. Repeat until the baking sheet is full, then bake the cookies for 16 to 18 minutes, or until the cookies are light brown and crispy. Continue making batches of cookies with the remaining dough.

• MAKES 100 COOKIES.

•   •   •   •

FRITOS
HOT BEAN DIP

☆   ✌   ●   ✐   ◉   ✄   ☞

Re-create the popular bean dip at home in just minutes with a food processor: Just pour in all the ingredients and fire it up. The best part about this recipe is that we can duplicate the taste of the popular dip without any added fat. If you check out the label of the real thing, you'll see that there's hydrogenated oil in there. We can avoid this saturated fat without sacrificing flavor with a home clone that's a perfect healthy choice for dipping. Bring on the chips!

One 15-ounce can pinto beans, drained
4 jalapeño pepper slices (bottled nacho slices)
1 tablespoon juice from bottled jalapeño pepper slices

$^1/_2$ teaspoon salt
$^1/_2$ teaspoon sugar
$^1/_4$ teaspoon onion powder
$^1/_4$ teaspoon paprika
$^1/_8$ teaspoon garlic powder
$^1/_8$ teaspoon cayenne pepper

Combine the drained pinto beans with the other ingredients in a food processor. Puree the ingredients on high speed until smooth. Transfer to a bowl, cover, and chill for at least 1 hour before serving.

• MAKES 1¼ CUPS.

•   •   •   •

HEINZ
PREMIUM CHILI SAUCE

The name of this tomato-based sauce belies its taste. There's not even a hint of spiciness here that someone might associate with "chili." Instead you get a sweet and sour sauce that's got more tang than ketchup, and more chunks. And what are those chunks? According to the label they're dehydrated onions, so that's exactly what we'll use in this formula. But be sure to get the kind that say dried "minced" onions, because dried "chopped" onions are too big. The recipe is a simple one since you just combine everything in a saucepan and simmer until done. And if you cruise down to the Tidbits at the bottom of this recipe, I'll show you a super-easy way to turn this saucy clone into a beautiful carbon copy of Heinz Seafood Cocktail Sauce.

I cup tomato puree	2 teaspoons granulated sugar
1/3 cup light corn syrup	I teaspoon salt
1/4 cup white vinegar	I teaspoon lemon juice
2 teaspoons dried minced onion	1/8 teaspoon garlic powder

Whisk together all the ingredients in a small saucepan and place it over medium-low heat. When the mixture begins to bubble, reduce the heat to low and simmer uncovered for 30 minutes. Cover and cool, then refrigerate until cold.

• MAKES I CUP.

Tidbits

You can easily bounce from this chili sauce into a clone of Heinz Seafood Cocktail Sauce by simply stirring in 2 teaspoons of prepared horseradish when the sauce has cooled. Cover and chill until needed.

• • • •

HELLMANN'S/BEST FOODS MAYONNAISE

☆   ✌   💣   ✎   ☯   ✂   ☞

One day in France in 1756, when Duke de Richelieu's chef couldn't find any cream for a sauce made with eggs and cream, he substituted oil. The thick emulsion that formed after a vigorous beating became one of the basic sauces for our modern cuisine. A version of this simple culinary breakthrough was an important ingredient for Richard Hellmann's salads in the deli he opened in New York City in 1905. When Richard started selling his mayonnaise by the jar at the deli, the bottles flew out the door. Before long Hellmann's creamy mayonnaise dominated in the eastern United States, while another company, Best Foods, was having incredible sales success with mayonnaise west of the Rockies. In 1932 Best Foods bought Hellmann's, and today the two brands split the country: Best Foods is sold west of the Rockies and Hellmann's can be found to the east. Nowadays the two mayonnaise recipes are nearly identical, although some people claim that Best Foods mayonnaise is a little tangier.

In this clone recipe you'll be creating an emulsion by whisking a stream of oil into a beaten egg yolk. The solution will begin to magically thicken and change color, and before you know it you'll be looking at a bowl of beautiful, off-white, fresh mayonnaise. I've found the best way to add the oil to the egg yolk a little bit at a time while whisking is to pour the oil into a plastic squirt bottle (like the kind used for ketchup or mustard). This will allow you to whisk continuously with one hand while squirting oil with the other. You can also use a measuring cup with a spout and pour the oil in a thin stream. The real stuff is made with soybean oil, which may not be available in your local market, but I found canola oil to be a great substitute.

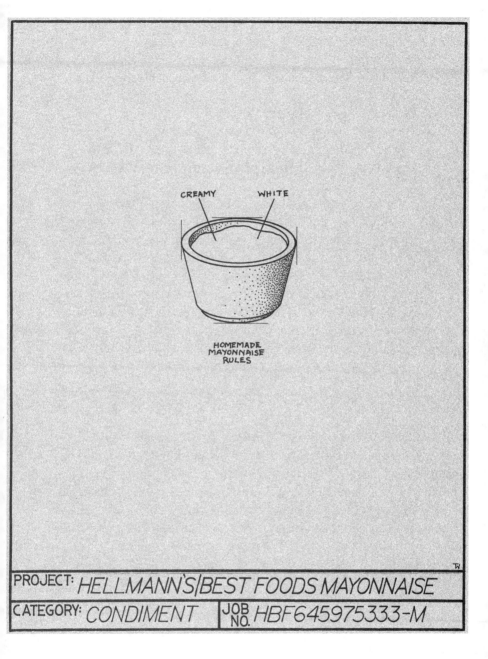

CREAMY WHITE

HOMEMADE
MAYONNAISE
RULES

PROJECT: *HELLMANN'S/BEST FOODS MAYONNAISE*

CATEGORY: *CONDIMENT* JOB NO. *HBF645975333-M*

1 egg yolk
2¼ teaspoons white vinegar
1 teaspoon water
¼ teaspoon plus ⅛ teaspoon salt

¼ teaspoon plus ⅛ teaspoon
  granulated sugar
¼ teaspoon lemon juice
1 cup soybean oil (or canola oil)

1. Whisk the egg yolk by hand for 15 seconds.
2. Combine the vinegar, water, salt, sugar, and lemon juice in a small bowl or glass measuring cup. Stir until the salt and sugar are dissolved. Add half this solution to the egg yolk and whisk for another 15 seconds.
3. Pour the oil into a plastic squirt bottle or a spouted measuring cup. Add a few drops of oil into the yolk and whisk, and continue to add oil a little bit at a time while whisking nonstop. When you have used about half the oil, your mayonnaise should be very thick. Add the remaining vinegar solution. Whisk some more. Now you can add the remaining oil in a steady stream while whisking until all the oil has been added. Your mayonnaise should be thick and off-white in color when it's done.
4. Put the mayonnaise into an old mayonnaise jar and seal it with a lid. Keep up to 2 weeks in your refrigerator.

• MAKES 1 CUP.

Tidbits

Some people are skeeved out by using raw egg yolk in a sauce like this, even though the risk of salmonella poisoning from fresh eggs is extremely low and the vinegar used in the recipe helps to kill any potentially harmful bacteria. Nevertheless, if you are concerned, you can buy eggs that have been heat-treated (pasteurized) in the shell. They are probably going to be a little more expensive.

HIDDEN VALLEY
THE ORIGINAL RANCH
DRESSING

☆   ✌   💣   ✏   ☯   ✂   ☞

Indeed, ranch dressing was invented at Hidden Valley Ranch near Santa Barbara, California, by a real salad-wranglin' rancher. In the '50s and '60s Steve Henson and his wife, Gayle, shared their 120-acre dude ranch with University of California at Santa Barbara students and other festive partiers for rousing weekend shindigs. The dozens of guests were served steak dinners and delicious salads topped with Steve's special blend of herbs, spices, mayonnaise, and buttermilk. As word got out about the fabulous dressing, more guests were showing up at the ranch and walking home with complimentary take-home jars filled with the stuff. Eventually Steve figured he could make a little cash on the side by packaging the dressing as a dry mix and selling it through the mail. At first he was filling envelopes himself, but within a few months Steve had to hire twelve more people to help with the packaging. Soon Steve had a multimillion-dollar business on his hands with a product that for ten years he had been giving away for free.

$\frac{1}{2}$ **cup mayonnaise**
$\frac{1}{2}$ **cup buttermilk**
$\frac{1}{4}$ **teaspoon dried parsley flakes**
$\frac{1}{4}$ **teaspoon ground black pepper**
$\frac{1}{4}$ **teaspoon MSG (such as Accent Flavor Enhancer)**

$\frac{1}{4}$ **teaspoon salt**
$\frac{1}{8}$ **teaspoon garlic powder**
$\frac{1}{8}$ **teaspoon onion powder**
pinch dried thyme

Combine all the ingredients in a medium bowl and whisk until smooth. Cover and chill for several hours before using.

• MAKES 1 CUP.

•   •   •   •

JACK IN THE BOX
PUMPKIN PIE SHAKE

☆　　✌　　💣　　✏　　☯　　✂　　☞

There's no need for artificial coloring or flavoring when re-creating this chain's delicious "limited-time only" holiday milkshake. Real canned pumpkin and pumpkin pie spices will do the trick in this Top Secret version. For the spices, rather than gathering up four costly bottles to use only a small amount from each, toss some pumpkin pie spice into your basket. It's a handy blend of cinnamon, ginger, nutmeg, and allspice that will be near the other spices in your market—McCormick makes a small size that's cheap. Combine everything below in a blender until smooth, and in a flash you've whipped up two servings of a delicious duplicate that can now be enjoyed any time of the year.

3/4 cup whole milk
3 tablespoons granulated
    sugar
3 cups vanilla ice cream

3/4 cup canned pumpkin (pure
    pumpkin)
3/4 teaspoon pumpkin pie spice

GARNISH
canned whipped cream

2 maraschino cherries

1. Dissolve the sugar in the milk in a measuring cup or small bowl.
2. Combine the milk and sugar mixture with the ice cream, pumpkin, and pumpkin pie spice in a blender on high speed. Blend until smooth, stir if necessary, and then pour the shake into two

16-ounce glasses. Garnish each with whipped cream and a cherry on top.

- MAKES TWO 16-OUNCE SHAKES.

•   •   •   •

JACQUIN'S
PEPPERMINT SCHNAPPS

☆   ✌   💣   ✎   ☯   ✂   ☞

All you need to make this minty schnapps at home is four ingredients, including inexpensive vodka, and an empty bottle to store it in. This is a recipe that was created for *More Top Secret Recipes* many years ago but didn't make it into the final version. Now it finally has a home.

¹/₃ cup granulated sugar
One 16-ounce bottle light corn
  syrup

2 cups 80-proof vodka
2 teaspoons peppermint extract

1. Combine the sugar and corn syrup in a 2-quart pan and place over medium heat. Heat until the sugar dissolves, stirring regularly, about 5 minutes.
2. When the sugar has dissolved, remove the mixture from the heat, add the vodka, and cover tightly with a lid. Let it cool down before you take off the lid.
3. When the liquid has cooled down, add the peppermint extract and pour it all into a sealable bottle.

- MAKES 4 CUPS.

• • • •

JASON'S DELI
CREAMY LIQUEUR FRUIT
DIPPING SAUCE

When Joe Tortorice and Rusty Coco opened the first Jason's Deli in Beaumont, Texas, in 1976, they could only dream of one day having more than 177 stores in 27 states. The original menu of twelve items has exploded to more than seventy-five, with many of the awesome sandwich selections paired up with a side order of assorted fruit and creamy liqueur fruit dipping sauce. The super-tasty sauce is easily cloned here with only three ingredients and can be customized for those of you watching the fat grams by substituting low-fat or fat-free sour cream. Serve this sauce along with a bowl of your favorite fresh fruit, such as pineapple, strawberries, grapes, or whatever happens to

1 cup sour cream
$^1/_2$ cup light brown sugar

4 teaspoons Grand Marnier
liqueur

be in season.

Whisk together all the ingredients in a medium bowl until the sugar is dissolved. Chill for 1 hour, then stir once before serving.

• MAKES 1 ½ CUPS.

• • • •

JIMMY DEAN
BREAKFAST SAUSAGE

☆ ✌ 💣 ✏ ☯ ✂ ☞

Before he became America's sausage king, Jimmy Dean was known for crooning the country hit "Big Bad John." That song came out in 1962 and sold more than 8 million copies. His singing success launched a television career on ABC with *The Jimmy Dean Show*, where Roy Clark, Patsy Cline, and Roger Miller got their big breaks. The TV exposure led to acting roles for Jimmy, as a regular on *Daniel Boone* and in feature films, including his debut in the James Bond flick *Diamonds Are Forever*. Realizing that steady income from an acting and singing career can be undependable, Jimmy invested his showbiz money in a hog farm. In 1968 the Jimmy Dean Meat Company developed a special recipe to transform those little piggies into the sausage that has now become a household name. Today the company is part of the Sara Lee Corporation, but Jimmy is still chairman of the board of his division at the age of eighty-one, although he was dropped as spokesman for the brand in 2004.

This clone recipe re-creates three varieties of the famous roll sausage that you form into patties and cook in a skillet. Use ground pork found at the supermarket (make it lean pork if you like), or grind some up yourself if you have a meat grinder laying around for some good old-fashioned fun.

REGULAR
16 ounces ground pork
1 teaspoon salt
1/2 teaspoon dried parsley

1/4 teaspoon rubbed dried sage
1/4 teaspoon ground black pepper
1/4 teaspoon dried thyme

$^1/_4$ teaspoon crushed red pepper
$^1/_4$ teaspoon ground coriander

$^1/_4$ teaspoon MSG (such as Accent Flavor Enhancer)

MAPLE

16 ounces ground pork
3 tablespoons maple-flavored syrup
1 teaspoon salt

$^1/_2$ teaspoon MSG (such as Accent Flavor Enhancer)
$^1/_4$ teaspoon ground coriander

HOT

16 ounces ground pork
1 teaspoon salt
$^1/_2$ teaspoon cayenne pepper
$^1/_4$ teaspoon rubbed dried sage
$^1/_4$ teaspoon ground black pepper

$^1/_4$ teaspoon crushed red pepper
$^1/_4$ teaspoon ground coriander
$^1/_4$ teaspoon MSG (such as Accent Flavor Enhancer)

Combine all the ingredients for the flavor of your choice in a medium bowl. Form the sausage into patties and cook in a skillet over medium heat until browned all over.

• EACH RECIPE MAKES 1 POUND OF SAUSAGE.

•   •   •   •

KFC
CAJUN HONEY WINGS

☆　　✌　　💣　　✒　　☯　　✂　　☞

When the "Limited-Time Only" signs came down for this one, I just smiled. These wings from KFC may be gone now, but with this clone that closely duplicates the sweet and spicy sauce on this amazing finger food, the great flavor of this recipe is here to stay. In each store the Colonel's peeps coat the wings with a KFC-style breading before frying them up and then tossing them in the delicious Cajun sauce. The sauce is da bomb on wings, but you can also put it to work on ribs or other chicken parts like breaded tenders or baked nuggets. This recipe calls for Emeril's Bayou Blast Cajun Seasoning, but it will also work with any other Cajun seasoning blend you score in your local market. Shortening works best for frying here, but you can also use vegetable oil.

SAUCE

$1/4$ cup ketchup
1 cup water
$3/4$ cup white vinegar
1 tablespoon vegetable oil
$1/3$ cup honey
4 teaspoons Emeril's Bayou Blast
　Cajun Seasoning

1 tablespoon minced canned
　green chiles
$1 1/4$ teaspoons chili powder
1 teaspoon minced garlic
$1/2$ teaspoon liquid smoke (hickory
　flavor)
$1/8$ teaspoon dried thyme

WINGS

6 to 10 cups vegetable
　shortening (or oil)
1 egg, beaten

1 cup milk
2 cups all-purpose flour
$2 1/2$ teaspoons salt

77

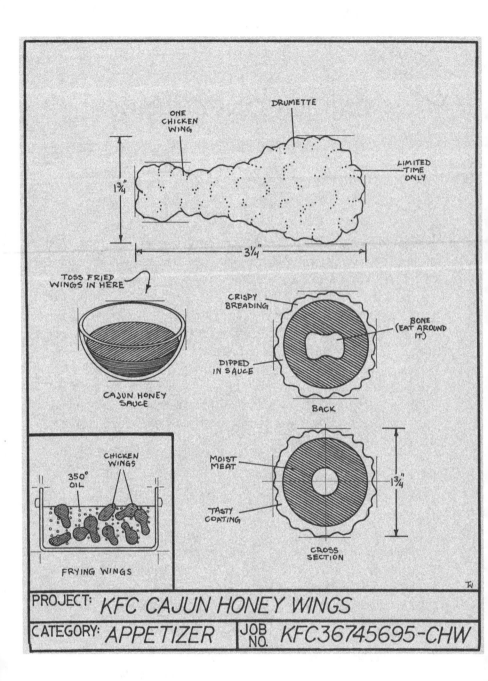

ONE CHICKEN WING

DRUMETTE

LIMITED TIME ONLY

1¾"

3¼"

TOSS FRIED WINGS IN HERE

CAJUN HONEY SAUCE

CRISPY BREADING

BONE (EAT AROUND IT)

DIPPED IN SAUCE

BACK

350° OIL

CHICKEN WINGS

FRYING WINGS

MOIST MEAT

TASTY COATING

1¾"

CROSS SECTION

TW

PROJECT:	*KFC CAJUN HONEY WINGS*	
CATEGORY: *APPETIZER*	JOB NO.	*KFC36745695-CHW*

³/₄ teaspoon ground black pepper
³/₄ teaspoon MSG (such as Accent
   Flavor Enhancer)

20 chicken wing pieces

1. Combine all the sauce ingredients in a small saucepan and place over medium heat. Stir until the ingredients are well combined and bring to a boil. Then reduce heat and simmer uncovered for 20 to 25 minutes, or until thickened.
2. As the sauce is simmering, heat up 6 to 10 cups of shortening or oil in a deep fryer set to 350 degrees F.
3. To make the wings, combine the beaten egg with the milk in a small bowl.
4. In another small bowl, combine the flour, salt, pepper, and MSG.
5. When the shortening is hot, dip each wing first in the flour mixture, then into the milk and egg mixture, and back into the flour. Arrange the wings on a plate until each one is coated with batter.
6. Fry the wings in the shortening or oil for 9 to 12 minutes, or until light golden brown. If you have a small fryer, you may wish to fry 10 of the wings at a time. Drain on paper towels or a rack.
7. When the sauce is done, brush the entire surface of each wing with a coating of sauce. Serve immediately.

- MAKES 2 TO 4 SERVINGS (20 WINGS).

KFC
CHICKEN POT PIE

☆　　✌　　💣　　✏　　👁　　✂　　☞

You know you're onto a bangin' pot pie when you knock through perfectly flaky crust to find just the right ratio of light and dark meat chicken and vegetables swimming in a deliciously creamy white sauce. KFC serves up a pie that totally fits the bill, and now I'm going to show you how to do exactly the same thing at home from scratch. You'll want to start this recipe a couple hours before you plan to bake the pies, since the dough for the crust should chill for a bit and the chicken needs to hang out in the brine to help make it moist and flavorful. When it comes time for baking, it's best to use small pie tins, ramekins, or Pyrex baking dishes (custard dishes) that hold 1½ cups of stuff. The recipe will then yield exactly 4 pot pies. If your baking dishes are smaller, there will still be enough dough here to make crust for up to 6 pot pies. And don't forget to brush leftover egg whites over the top of the pies before you pop them into the oven to get the same shiny crust as the original.

DOUGH

1½ cups all-purpose flour
½ teaspoon salt
5 tablespoons cold butter

¼ cup shortening
3 tablespoons cold water
2 eggs, separated

CHICKEN

4 cups water
3 tablespoons salt

2 tablespoons sugar
1 teaspoon ground black pepper

¾ *pound chicken breast fillets*
(about 2 fillets)

½ *pound chicken thigh fillets*
(about 2 fillets)

FILLING

1 *cup sliced carrots (about 2*
  small carrots)
1 *cup diced russet potato (about*
  ½ *medium potato)*
1 *cup frozen peas*
¼ *cup butter*

¼ *cup all-purpose flour*
1 ½ *cups chicken broth*
1 *cup whole milk*
½ *teaspoon salt*
¼ *teaspoon rubbed dried sage*
pinch ground black pepper

1. Make the dough for the crust by combining the flour and salt in a medium bowl. Use a fork or a pastry knife to cut the cold butter and shortening into the flour until there are no pieces of butter or shortening larger than peas. Add the water and egg yolks (save the egg whites for later), and bring the dough together with your hands until you can form it into a ball. Wrap the ball in plastic and let it chill out in the fridge for 2 hours.
2. Make the brine for the chicken by combining the water with the salt, sugar, and ground black pepper. Stir until the sugar and salt dissolve, and then add the chicken, cover, and chill for 2 hours. Don't let the chicken marinate for more than 2 hours or it will be too salty. If you will not be using the chicken after it has brined for exactly 2 hours, remove it from the brine and rinse it off, and then pop it back into the fridge inside a storage bag or covered container until you need it.
3. When you are ready to assemble the pot pies, preheat the oven to 400 degrees F.
4. Preheat a sauté pan drizzled with about 1 tablespoon vegetable oil over medium heat. Rinse the chicken fillets, and then dry them. Add the chicken fillets to the pan and sauté the breasts for 5 to 6 minutes per side and the thighs for 3 to 4 minutes per side. Remove the chicken and let it cool, then tear it into bite-size pieces.
5. Use a steamer basket in a covered pan over boiling water to steam the sliced carrots and diced potato for 6 minutes. Add frozen peas and steam for an additional 6 minutes.

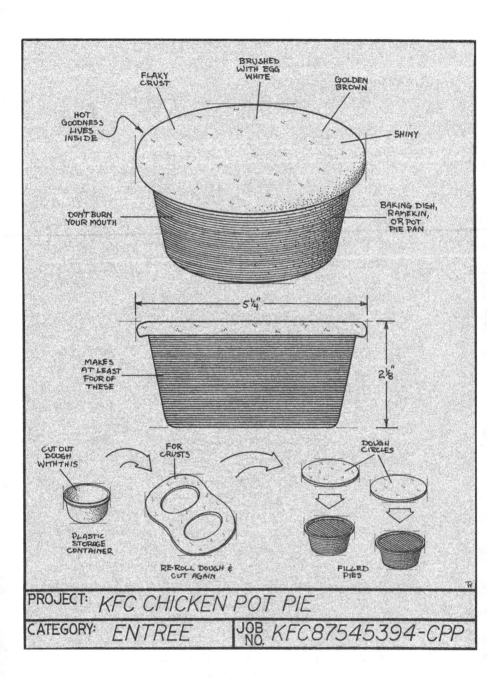

FLAKY CRUST

BRUSHED WITH EGG WHITE

GOLDEN BROWN

HOT GOODNESS LIVES INSIDE

SHINY

DON'T BURN YOUR MOUTH

BAKING DISH, RAMEKIN, OR POT PIE PAN

5 1/4"

MAKES AT LEAST FOUR OF THESE

2 1/8"

CUT OUT DOUGH WITH THIS

FOR CRUSTS

DOUGH CIRCLES

PLASTIC STORAGE CONTAINER

RE-ROLL DOUGH & CUT AGAIN

FILLED PIES

PROJECT: *KFC CHICKEN POT PIE*

CATEGORY: *ENTREE*

JOB NO. *KFC87545394-CPP*

6. Make the sauce by melting the butter over medium-low heat in a large saucepan. Whisk in the flour, turn the heat to medium, and cook the flour and butter mixture for 1 minute, whisking often. Add the chicken broth and milk while whisking and simmer for 5 minutes, or until the sauce thickens. Add the steamed vegetables, chicken, salt, sage, and ground black pepper. Turn off the heat and allow the filling to cool for 10 minutes.

7. Build the pot pies by spooning 1 to 1½ cups of filling into small baking dishes, ramekins, or aluminum pot pie pans. Fill all the pot pie pans and then get the dough ready.

8. Roll out dough and cut it into circles using an inverted round plastic storage container that has a diameter about 1 inch larger than the pie pans. You can roll the dough circles more after you cut them out if you need to stretch them bigger. Place the dough over each pie and then pinch all the way around the edges to seal. Slightly beat the leftover egg whites and brush over the top of each pot pie. Place the pies on a baking sheet and bake for 22 to 25 minutes, or until the tops are golden brown.

- MAKES 4 TO 6 POT PIES.

• • • •

KOZY SHACK
RICE PUDDING

☆　　✌　　💣　　✏　　☯　　✂　　☞

Once deliveryman Vinnie Gruppuso tasted the pudding being made at one of the delis in Brooklyn that he delivered bread to back in the 1960s, he was hooked. He eventually struck up a deal with that deli—called Cozy Shack—to sell the pudding to other customers on his route, and the product soon outsold his other delivery items. Eventually Vinnie scrapped up enough money to purchase the deli's pudding operation, he changed the "C" in the name to a "K," and today Kozy Shack is the number one manufacturer of rice pudding in North America. Just as in the original secret formula, six basic ingredients are all that go into this clone of the company's top seller. But you'll also need a cooking thermometer and a large pot with at least a 10-inch diameter. A pot this wide helps the mixture to reduce faster, and the milk won't be so deep as to obscure the readings on mercury thermometers. Keep your eye on the temperature and be sure to stir the pudding often. When the mixture begins to thicken, pop the pudding into your fridge for several hours, where it will continue to thicken to the creamy consistency of the real thing as it cools.

½ gallon whole milk
⅔ cup granulated sugar
1 egg, beaten
¼ teaspoon salt

⅔ cup medium-grain rice
 (uncooked)
½ teaspoon vanilla extract

1. Combine the milk with the sugar, beaten egg, and salt in a large pot and place over medium heat. Bring the temperature up to

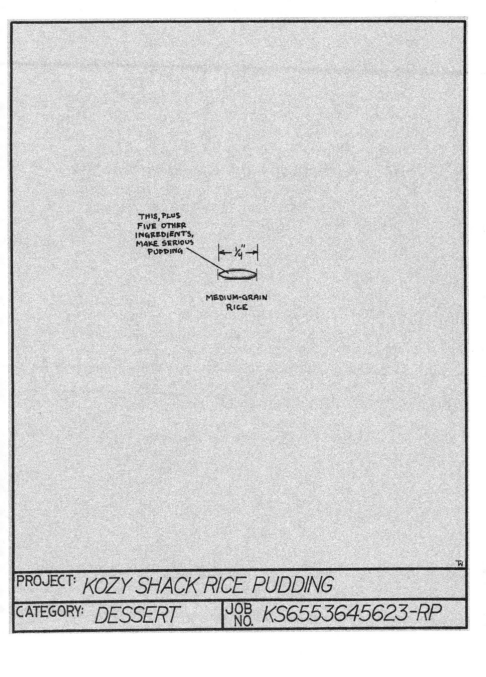

THIS, PLUS
FIVE OTHER
INGREDIENTS,
MAKE SERIOUS
PUDDING

|← ¼" →|

MEDIUM-GRAIN
RICE

TW

PROJECT: *KOZY SHACK RICE PUDDING*

CATEGORY: *DESSERT*   JOB NO. *KS6553645623-RP*

exactly 160 degrees F, while stirring often. This should take 10 to 15 minutes.

2. Stir in the rice and continue heating the mixture until it simmers at 185 to 190 degrees F. When the mixture begins to bubble, maintain 185 to 190 degrees F (reduce the heat if necessary) and continue cooking for 35 to 40 minutes, or until the pudding thickens. Be sure to stir the mixture often so that the rice doesn't stick to the bottom of the pan. When the pudding begins to thicken, turn off the heat and stir in the vanilla. Cool the pudding in the pot uncovered for 10 minutes, and then pour it into a wide container, cover, and refrigerate it for several hours before serving. The rice pudding will continue to thicken as it chills.

• Makes 7 cups.

Tidbits

There are actually very few whole grains of rice in Kozy Shack Rice Pudding. For an even better clone, run the raw rice grains through a food processor on high speed for about a minute or until you see the grains breaking into smaller bits. Pour these rice pieces (and any dust created from the process, since it will work as an additional thickener), into the pudding in step #2 as described above.

• • • •

KRAFT MIRACLE WHIP

Even though this stuff looks like mayonnaise, Food and Drug Administration dudes say it has to be called "dressing." Miracle Whip was invented in 1933 as a sweeter, more flavorful alternative to mayonnaise, but it contains a few extra ingredients that the FDA says aren't supposed to be in mayonnaise, such as sugar, paprika, and garlic powder. If you're a fan of Kraft's variation on the creamy white mother sauce, you must try this clone. As with homemade mayonnaise, you make a simple emulsion with egg yolk and oil. Add in the other ingredients and you've got yourself a Miracle Whip kitchen copy that's way fresher than any bottle on store shelves.

1 egg yolk
5 teaspoons white vinegar
4 teaspoons granulated sugar
1/4 teaspoon plus 1/8 teaspoon salt
1/4 teaspoon lemon juice

1 cup canola oil
1/4 teaspoon dry mustard
pinch paprika
pinch garlic powder

1. Whisk the egg yolk by hand for 15 seconds.
2. Combine the vinegar, sugar, salt, and lemon juice in a small bowl or glass measuring cup. Stir until the salt and sugar are dissolved. Add half this solution to the egg yolk and whisk for another 15 seconds.
3. Pour the canola oil into a plastic squirt bottle or measuring cup with a spout. This will allow you to drizzle the oil into the egg yolk with one hand while whisking with the other. Dribble a few drops of oil into the yolk and whisk, and continue to add oil a

little bit at a time while whisking nonstop. When you are about halfway through the oil, your mayonnaise should be very thick. Whisk in the remaining vinegar solution and add the mustard, paprika, and garlic powder. Now you can add the remaining oil in a steady stream while whisking until all of the oil has been added.

4. Put the dressing into an old mayonnaise jar and seal it with a lid. Keep up to 7 to 10 days in your refrigerator.

• MAKES 1 CUP.

Tidbits

If you are concerned about the raw egg yolk used in this recipe (even though the risk of salmonella poisoning from well-chilled fresh eggs is extremely low), you can buy eggs that have been heat-treated (pasteurized) for a bit more scratch. The vinegar used in the recipe also helps kill any stray bacteria baddies.

• • • •

KRISPY KREME
ORIGINAL GLAZED
DOUGHNUTS

☆　　　✌　　　💣　　　✏　　　☯　　　✂　　　☞

The specifics of the well-guarded, seventy-two-year-old secret recipe for Krispy Kreme doughnuts may be securely locked away in a safe at the Winston-Salem, North Carolina, headquarters, but discovering the basic ingredients in these puffy, fried cakes of joy was far from impossible. Simply asking to see the ingredients listed on the dry doughnut mix was all it took. Nevertheless, knowing the exact ingredients in a Krispy Kreme glazed doughnut is hardly all the information one needs to clone America's most popular glazed doughnut at home.

The automated process for creating Krispy Kreme doughnuts, developed in the 1950s, took the company many years to perfect. When you drive by your local Krispy Kreme store between 5:00 and 11:00 each day (both a.m. and p.m.) and see the "Hot Doughnuts Now" sign lit up, inside the store custom-made stainless-steel machines are rolling. Doughnut batter is extruded into little doughnut shapes that ride up and down through a temperature and humidity controlled booth to activate the yeast. This creates the perfect amount of air in the dough that will yield a tender and fluffy finished product. When the doughnuts are perfectly puffed up, they're gently dumped into a moat of hot vegetable shortening where they float on one side until golden brown, and then the machine flips them over to cook the other side. When the doughnuts finish frying, they ride up a mesh conveyer belt and through a ribbon of white sugar glaze. If you're lucky enough to taste one of these doughnuts just as it comes around the corner from the glazing, you're in for a real treat—the warm circle of sweet doughy goodness practically melts in your mouth. It's this secret process that helped Krispy Kreme become the fastest-growing doughnut chain in the country.

As you can guess, the main ingredient in a Krispy Kreme doughnut is wheat flour, but there is also some added gluten, soy flour, malted barley flour, and modified food starch; plus egg yolk, nonfat milk, flavoring, and yeast. I suspect a low-gluten flour, like cake flour, is probably used in the original mix to make the doughnuts tender, and then the manufacturer adds the additional gluten to give the doughnuts the perfect framework for rising. I tested many combinations of cake flour and wheat gluten but found that the best texture resulted from cake flour combined with all-purpose flour. I also tried adding a little soy flour to the mix, but the soy gave the dough a strange taste and it didn't benefit the texture of the dough in any way. I also excluded the malted barley flour and modified food starch from the recipe since these are difficult ingredients to find. These exclusions didn't seem to matter because the real secret in making these doughnuts look and taste like the original lies primarily in careful handling of the dough. The dough will be very sticky when first mixed together, and you should be careful not to overmix it or you will build up some tough gluten strands, and that will result in chewy doughnuts. You don't even need to touch the dough until it is finished with the first rising stage. After the dough rises for 30 to 45 minutes it will become easier to handle, but you will still need to flour your hands. Also, be sure to generously flour the surface you are working on when you gently roll out the dough for cutting. When each doughnut shape is cut from the dough, place it onto a small square of wax paper that has been lightly dusted with flour. Using wax paper will allow you to easily transport the doughnuts (after they rise) from the baking sheet to the hot shortening without deflating the dough. As long as you don't fry them too long—1 minute per side should be enough—you will have tender homemade doughnuts that will satisfy even the biggest Krispy Kreme fanatics.

Since we are making these doughnuts by hand without some of the uncommon ingredients found in Krispy Kreme doughnuts today, it's likely that this clone formula creates doughnuts more like the original Krispy Kreme recipe, which founder Vernon Rudolph purchased from a New Orleans chef in 1937. That's long before machines took over the process.

3/4 cup warm water (100 to 110 degrees F)

1 package (2 1/4 teaspoons) active dry yeast

2 teaspoons granulated sugar

1 cup all-purpose flour

3/4 cup plus 1 tablespoon cake flour

3/4 teaspoon salt

1 egg yolk

1 tablespoon nonfat milk

1/2 teaspoon vanilla extract

GLAZE

1/3 cup water

3/4 cup granulated sugar

1/2 cup powdered sugar

1/4 teaspoon meringue powder

pinch salt

6 to 10 cups vegetable shortening (as required by your fryer)

1. Dissolve the yeast and sugar in the warm water. Let solution stand for 5 minutes or until it becomes foamy on top. Make sure the water isn't too hot to avoid killing the yeast.

2. Sift the flour and salt together into a large bowl. Beat egg yolk in a small bowl, then stir in the milk and vanilla. Pour the yeast solution into the bowl with the egg and milk, and stir. Make a well in the center of the flour, then pour the yeast solution into that well. Stir by hand gently with a wooden spoon from the middle, slowly bringing in more flour until all ingredients come together into a ball—the dough will still be too sticky to handle at this point. Cover the bowl and let it sit in a warm place for 30 to 45 minutes or until the dough doubles in size.

3. While the dough is rising, cut ten 4 x 4-inch squares of wax paper and arrange them on two rimmed baking sheets. Each doughnut will rise on its own square of wax paper, and the rimmed baking sheet will allow you to wrap a large sheet of foil over the doughnuts without the foil touching the doughnuts. Sprinkle a little flour on each of the squares of wax paper.

4. Use flour on your hands to transfer the dough to a floured surface. Sprinkle a little flour on top of the dough, and then gently

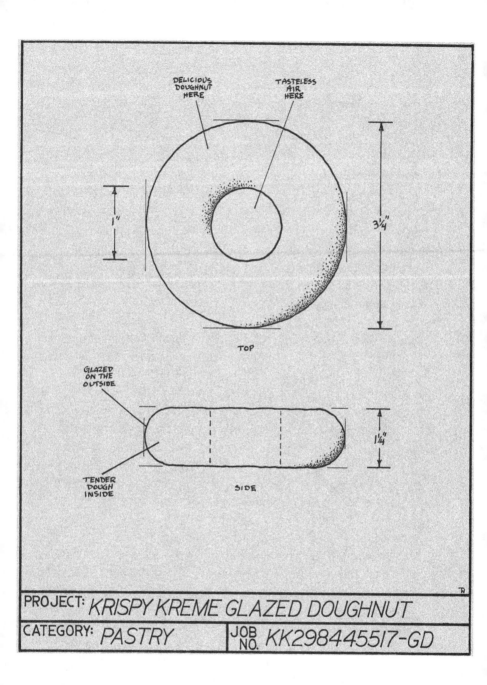

DELICIOUS
DOUGHNUT
HERE

TASTELESS
AIR
HERE

1"

3¼"

TOP

GLAZED
ON THE
OUTSIDE

1¼"

TENDER
DOUGH
INSIDE

SIDE

PROJECT: *KRISPY KREME GLAZED DOUGHNUT*

CATEGORY: *PASTRY*   JOB NO. *KK298445517-GD*

roll out the dough until it's about ½ inch thick. Use only the amount of flour needed to allow you to handle the dough. Use a 3-inch biscuit cutter to cut out circles of dough, then use a lid from a plastic soda or water bottle (about 1⅛-ich diameter) to cut the holes. Carefully place each doughnut on a square of wax paper with the most floured side of the doughnut down on the wax paper. Cover the doughnuts with large sheets of foil and let them sit for 45 minutes in a warm place until the doughnuts have puffed up to at least twice their original size.

5. While the doughnuts rest, make the glaze by combining water and granulated sugar in a small saucepan over medium heat. Bring mixture to a boil and then reduce heat and simmer for 1 minute, or until the solution is clear. Pour hot sugar solution into a medium mixing bowl, add the powdered sugar, meringue powder, and a pinch of salt, then use an electric mixture and mix for 2 minutes on high speed. Cover this bowl with plastic wrap until you need it.

6. As the doughnuts rise, heat vegetable shortening in a fryer to 375 degrees F.

7. When the doughnuts have doubled in size, carefully transfer 2 or 3 doughnuts at a time to the hot shortening. Turn each doughnut over onto the palm of your hand, carefully remove the wax paper, and then drop it into the oil. Fry for 1 minute, flip the doughnut with the handle of a wooden spoon, and continue frying for an additional minute. Remove doughnuts to a cooling rack for one minute.

8. After a minute on the cooking rack, spoon the glaze over the top of each doughnut so that it runs down the sides and off onto the plate below the cooling rack. In between each glazing stir the glaze so that it stays smooth. If the glaze begins to thicken, stir in just a little bit of hot water to thin it out. Let the glazed doughnuts cool for at least 5 minutes before eating. Don't store doughnuts in a sealed container or moisture from the doughnuts will melt the glaze. Instead, store them covered loosely with aluminum foil. Stored this way the doughnuts will be good for about 1 day.

• MAKES 10 DOUGHNUTS.

• • • •

LAWRY'S
RED PEPPER SEASONED SALT
(MADE WITH TABASCO)

The spicy seasoned salt mash-up that Lawry's and Tabasco created several years ago garnered a cult following. Unfortunately the number of fanatics that celebrated the delicious salty, sour, and spicy blend was too small to satisfy the manufacturer, and today this tasty blend has joined my growing list of Dead Foods. The good news is—after much tinkering in the Top Secret Lab—I've discovered a technique for a home version, and the process is a simple one. We can duplicate the sourness that comes from vinegar powder in the real thing by adding Tabasco pepper sauce, which contains vinegar, to a handful of dry ingredients and then letting the blend dry overnight. The hardened chunks are then ground with a mortar and pestle or a coffee grinder, producing a fine blend that can be poured into a spice shaker and sprinkled on anything from french fries to eggs. It's back!

1 1/2 tablespoons salt
2 teaspoons granulated sugar
1 teaspoon cayenne pepper
1/4 teaspoon paprika
1/4 teaspoon garlic powder

1/4 teaspoon onion powder
1/4 teaspoon ground black pepper
1/8 teaspoon sour salt (citric
    acid—see Tidbits)
1 teaspoon Tabasco pepper sauce

1. Combine all the ingredients except the Tabasco pepper sauce in a small bowl.
2. Add the Tabasco and stir well, then spread the mixture onto a plate and let it dry overnight. Stir the mixture occasionally as it dries.

3. When the seasoning blend is completely dry, use a mortar and pestle to grind the hardened chunks down to a finer blend that will pass through a wire-mesh strainer. You can also pulse the mixture in a coffee grinder until all the chunks are pulverized. Pour the blend into an empty spice shaker and sprinkle on your food with glee.

- MAKES ABOUT ¼ CUP OR 1.75 OUNCES.

Tidbits
Citric acid is an important ingredient that gives the blend its lemony tang. You can typically find this white crystalline substance—which is also called "sour salt"—in the aisle where ethnic or Jewish foods are located in your market.

•　•　•　•

LIPTON
BRISK ICED TEA

I found a great secret ingredient to duplicate the lemony tartness in a can of Brisk Iced Tea. Kool-Aid unsweetened lemonade drink mix has the perfect mixture of citric acid and lemon juice solids to help you effortlessly clone this one over and over again by the pitcher, as your thirst demands.

3 Lipton tea bags (regular size)
1 cup plus 2 tablespoons
  granulated sugar

½ teaspoon Kool-Aid lemonade
  unsweetened drink mix

1. Bring 2 quarts of water to a boil in a large saucepan. Add the tea bags and remove the pan from the heat. Let the tea steep for at least 1 hour.
2. Pour the granulated sugar and Kool-Aid drink mix into a 2-quart pitcher. Add the tea and stir until the sugar dissolves. Add additional water if necessary to bring the tea to the 2-quart mark on the pitcher. Chill well before serving.

• MAKES 2 QUARTS.

•   •   •   •

LIPTON DIET GREEN TEA WITH CITRUS

☆　　✂　　●　　✏　　◐　　✂　　☞

I was having trouble getting the flavors just right for Lipton's bottled diet green tea, which has become such a big seller these days. Real lime juice wasn't cutting it, nor were any of the extracts or oils I tried. Then, one day, I stumbled onto a new product called True Lime. It's a crystallized lime substitute that's made with lime juice and lime oil, and it comes in 2.85-ounce bottles or in boxes of 40 packets. It can be found in the baking aisle of your local supermarket, and it can be used for cooking wherever lime juice is required, or you can dissolve it in beverages. Had I found my secret ingredient? After some experimenting, I discovered that the citric acid in True Lime adds just the right amount of acidic tang that we need for a clone that tastes like the original product (which also contains citric acid). Success! To make your own version of this popular bottled green tea, simply pour some boiling water over a couple of green tea bags, add the other ingredients listed below, and you'll soon have a home-brewed clone of Lipton's hit drink. Calories not included.

4 cups boiling water
2 green tea bags (Lipton brand is best)
2½ teaspoons Equal (10 single-serving packets)

1¼ teaspoons True Lime
¼ teaspoon orange extract

1. Pour the boiling water over the tea bags and steep for 1 hour.
2. Combine the tea and remaining ingredients in a pitcher, whisk to dissolve the Equal, and chill well before serving.

- MAKES 1 QUART.

• • • •

LINCOLN SNACKS
POPPYCOCK

☆　　　✌　　　💣　　　✏　　　☯　　　✂　　　☞

This Nebraska-based company grows a special kind of yellow mushroom popcorn that pops into fluffy round shapes for all its brands of candy-coated popcorn—Fiddle Faddle, Screaming Yellow Zonkers, and Poppycock—but plain microwave popcorn is all you'll need to make an easy clone. The Poppycock motto is "It's our amazing glaze!" and it is pretty amazing. The butter-toffee glaze is flavored with maple syrup, and each box is packed with lots of nuts, unlike any other glazed popcorn brands out there. Clone the Poppycock flavor you prefer: all cashews, all pecans, or a combination of almonds and pecans. Of course, you can mix in any nuts you like, salted or unsalted, as long as it comes to two cups' worth (for example, macadamia nuts is an awesome variation). You really need a candy thermometer for this recipe to get it just right, but you can also estimate temperature by drizzling some of the candy syrup into a glass of cold water once you see it begin to darken. If the candy forms brittle threads, it's ready. You coat the popcorn with the glaze by heating everything up in the microwave and stirring. There is also a technique using your oven (see Tidbits), but the microwave method is faster.

¾ cup light corn syrup

½ cup light brown sugar

2 tablespoons granulated sugar

½ cup butter (salted)

⅓ cup maple syrup

¼ cup water

¼ teaspoon salt

1 teaspoon vanilla extract

8 cups plain (not buttered) popped microwave popcorn

2 cups nuts (pecans, cashews, or almonds/pecans)

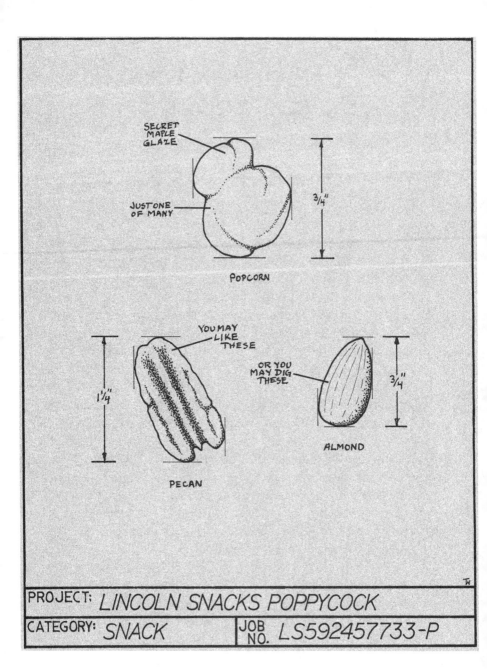

SECRET
MAPLE
GLAZE

JUST ONE
OF MANY

3/4"

POPCORN

YOU MAY
LIKE
THESE

OR YOU
MAY DIG
THESE

3/4"

1¼"

PECAN

ALMOND

PROJECT: *LINCOLN SNACKS POPPYCOCK*

CATEGORY: *SNACK*

JOB NO. *LS592457733-P*

100

1. Combine the corn syrup, sugars, butter, maple syrup, water, and salt in a large saucepan and place over medium heat. Simmer the mixture and monitor it with a candy thermometer. Your target temperature is 290 degrees F, or just before the hard crack stage. The temperature continues to rise a bit after you turn off the heat, so this is a good place to stop cooking.
2. While the candy cooks, pop the popcorn in the microwave and measure out 8 cups of popcorn. Make sure to remove any unpopped kernels. Pour the popcorn into a large microwave-safe glass bowl. Measure the nuts of your choice into a glass measuring cup. Just before the candy reaches 290 degrees F, microwave the nuts in the measuring cup on high for 1 minute to warm them up.
3. When your candy hits 290 degrees F, turn off the heat, add the vanilla, and stir in the warm nuts. Immediately microwave the bowl of popped popcorn for 1 minute on high, then pour the candy and nuts mixture over the popcorn while stirring. Microwave the bowl for 1 more minute on high, then stir well to coat the popcorn and nuts with candy. You may want to go back into the microwave for an additional minute since the candy will begin to harden quickly. Stir well to coat all the popcorn, then quickly pour the popcorn out onto wax paper or a silicone mat.
4. When the popcorn has cooled, break it up and put it into a tightly sealed container to keep it fresh. This stuff gets sticky and stale pretty quickly in moist climates.

- MAKES 10 CUPS.

Tidbits

To use your oven rather than the microwave to coat the popcorn and nuts, preheat it to 275 degrees F while the candy is cooking. Pour the nuts on a large buttered baking sheet. When the candy reaches 290 degrees F, add the vanilla, then stir the warm nuts into the candy. Spread the popcorn on the baking sheet, drizzle with the hot candy syrup, and stir. Put the popcorn back into the oven for 5 minutes, then take it out and stir to coat. Repeat if necessary, pour onto wax paper or a silicone mat, then go to step #4.

MAID-RITE
LOOSE MEAT SANDWICH

☆   ✌   💣   ✐   🎱   ✂   ☞

It's been an Iowa tradition since 1926, and today this sandwich has a huge cult following. It's similar to a traditional hamburger, but the ground beef is not formed into a patty. Instead, the lightly seasoned meat lies uncompressed on a white bun, dressed with mustard, minced onion, and dill pickles. Since the meat is loose, the sandwich is always served with a spoon for scooping up the ground beef that will inevitably fall out.

When this clone recipe for Maid-Rite was originally posted on our Web site several years ago, it elicited more e-mail than any recipe in the site's history. Numerous Midwesterners were keyboard-ready to insist that the clone was far from accurate without the inclusion of a few bizarre ingredients, the most common of which was Coca-Cola. One letter states: "You evidently have not ever had a Maid-Rite. The secret to the Maid-Rite is coke syrup. Without it you cannot come close to the taste." Another e-mail reads: "Having lived in the Midwest all of my life and knowing not only the owners of a Maid-Rite restaurant but also many people who worked there, I can tell you that one of the things you left out of your recipe is Coca-Cola. Not a lot, just enough to keep the meat moist."

On the flip side, I received comments such as this one from an Iowa fan who lived near Don Taylor's original Maid-Rite franchise: "The secret to the best Maid-Rite is the whole beef. Don had a butcher shop in his basement where he cut and ground all his beef. Some people still swear they added seasoning, but that is just not true. Not even pepper."

Back in the underground lab, no matter how hard I examined the meat in the original product—which I had shipped in dry ice directly from Don Taylor's original store in Marshalltown, Iowa—I could not detect Coca-Cola. There's no sweetness to the meat at all, although the buns themselves seem to include some sugar (when the buns are chewed with the meat, the sandwich does taste mildly sweet). I finally concluded that Coca-Cola syrup is not part of the recipe. If it is added to the meat in the Maid-Rite stores, it's an insignificant amount that does not have any noticeable effect on the flavor.

Also, the texture is important, so adding plenty of liquid to the simmering meat is crucial. This clone recipe requires 1 cup of water in addition to ¼ cup of beef broth. By simmering the ground beef in this liquid for a couple of hours, we'll break down the meat to tenderize it and infuse a little flavor, just like the real thing.

When the liquid is gone, form the ground beef into a ½ cup measuring scoop, dump it onto the bottom of a plain hamburger bun, then add your choice of mustard, onions, and pickles. Adding ketchup is up to you, although it's not an ingredient found in Maid-Rite stores. Many say that back in the early days, "hobos" would swipe the ketchup and mix it with water to make tomato soup. Free ketchup was nixed from the restaurants way back then, and the custom has been in place ever since.

1 pound lean ground beef	*4 plain hamburger buns*
(15% fat is best)	*yellow mustard*
1 cup water	*minced white onion*
¼ cup beef broth	*dill pickle slices*
¼ teaspoon salt	

1. Brown the ground beef in a large skillet with a lid over medium-low heat. Use a potato masher to help get the ground beef into small pieces. Drain any excess fat. If you use lean meat (15% fat or less), you won't need to drain the fat. As soon as all the pink in the meat is gone, add the water, beef broth, and salt. Cover the meat and simmer for 2 hours, or until all the liquid is gone, stirring every 10 minutes or so. If the liquid is not gone after 2 hours, continue cooking the meat uncovered until the liquid is gone.

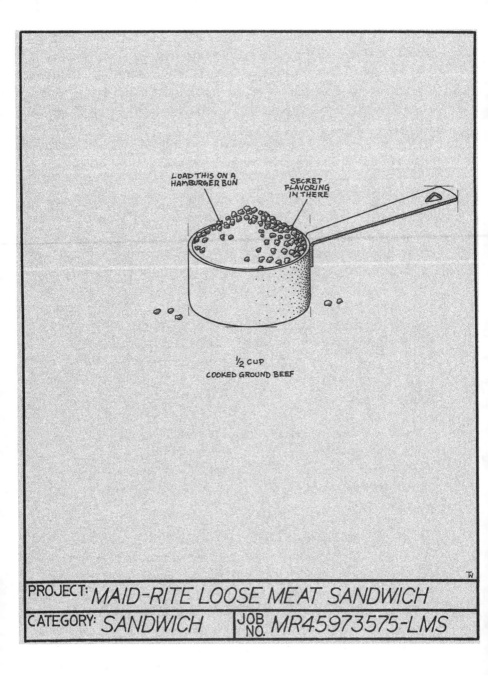

LOAD THIS ON A
HAMBURGER BUN

SECRET
FLAVORING
IN THERE

½ CUP
COOKED GROUND BEEF

PROJECT: MAID-RITE LOOSE MEAT SANDWICH

CATEGORY: SANDWICH   JOB NO. MR45973575-LMS

2. Build each sandwich by pressing the hot ground beef into a ½ cup measuring cup. Dump the meat onto the bottom of a plain hamburger bun. Add mustard to the top half of the bun, along with minced onion and pickles if desired. Put the sandwich together, and heat it up in your microwave oven for 10 to 15 seconds to warm the buns. Serve with a spoon as they do in the restaurants.

- MAKES 4 SANDWICHES.

• • • •

MARS
MUNCH BAR

☆   ✌   💣   ✏   ☯   ✂   ☞

At one point Mars, Inc., chose to capitalize on the company's best-selling candy bar, and called this one Snickers Munch Bar. I think that may have been confusing to consumers who expected to open the wrapper and find something inside resembling a Snickers bar. Other than the abundance of peanuts in this butter toffee brittle, this candy bar is nothing like Snickers. It is, however, an awesome peanut brittle that's super-easy to clone. The original is made with only six ingredients: peanuts, sugar, butter, corn syrup, salt, and soy lecithin. The soy lecithin is an emulsifier used here for texture, but this ingredient is hard to find, and we really don't need it for a good clone. Use a candy thermometer to bring the mixture of sugar, butter, and corn syrup up to 300 degrees F, then pour it over warmed, salted peanuts. When the candy has cooled, break it into chunks and you will have created the equivalent of 12 bars of the addicting original.

2 cups salted dry-roasted
   peanuts
¹/₂ cup butter (1 stick, salted)

¹/₂ cup granulated sugar
¹/₄ cup light corn syrup

1. Spread the peanuts out on a nonstick baking sheet and heat them up in your oven set on 300 degrees F. This will warm up the peanuts so that they don't cool the candy too quickly when added later. There's no need to preheat the oven.
2. Melt the butter in a medium saucepan over medium-low heat.
3. Add the sugar and corn syrup and simmer, stirring occasionally. Put a candy thermometer in the mixture and watch it closely.

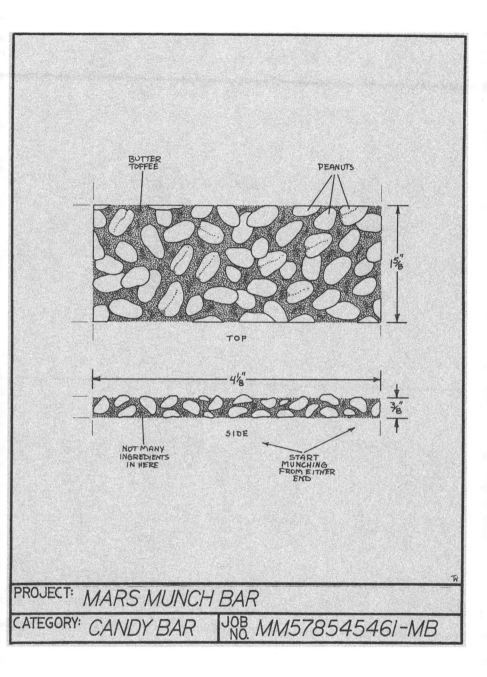

BUTTER
TOFFEE

PEANUTS

1⅝"

TOP

4⅛"

⅜"

SIDE

NOT MANY
INGREDIENTS
IN HERE

START
MUNCHING
FROM EITHER
END

PROJECT: *MARS MUNCH BAR*

CATEGORY: *CANDY BAR* **JOB NO.** *MM578545461-MB*

4. When the mixture reaches 300 degrees F, add the peanuts and stir well until all of the peanuts are coated with candy. Pour the candy onto the warm baking sheet and spread it flat. When the candy cools, break it into chunks and store it in a covered container.

- MAKES THE EQUIVALENT OF TWELVE 1.5-OUNCE CANDY BARS.

• • • •

MAUNA LOA
KONA COFFEE GLAZED
MACADAMIAS

☆ ✌ 💣 🖊 ☯ ✂ ☞

It's not necessary to use expensive Kona coffee when cloning these awesome glazed macadamia nuts from Mauna Loa. Since the coffee is combined with butter, sugar, and other ingredients, no one will know the difference. But you will have to make your coffee very strong. Use twice the grounds recommended by your coffeemaker or use espresso for this recipe. You'll also need a candy thermometer since you'll need to bring the candy to precisely 290 degrees F before stirring in the nuts. Make sure to heat up the nuts in a separate pan so they'll be hot when you add them to the candy. This way the candy doesn't cool too quickly and the nuts get a nice thin coating of the goodness. The candy coating won't be as thin as on the original nuts, but it's a pretty good copy considering your home kitchen probably doesn't come equipped with one of the commercial candy tumblers or enrobers you find on the production line in the Mauna Loa manufacturing plant.

3 cups dry-roasted macadamia
  nuts (two 6-ounce jars)
$^1/_2$ cup strong coffee or espresso
$^1/_3$ cup granulated sugar
$^1/_4$ cup dark brown sugar

$^1/_4$ cup light corn syrup
$^1/_4$ cup ($^1/_2$ stick) butter
$^1/_4$ teaspoon salt
$^1/_2$ teaspoon vanilla extract

1. Pour the macadamia nuts into a large skillet and place over medium-low heat. This will make the nuts hot so that the candy will coat better. The nuts should get hot, but don't let them brown. If they start to brown, turn off the heat.

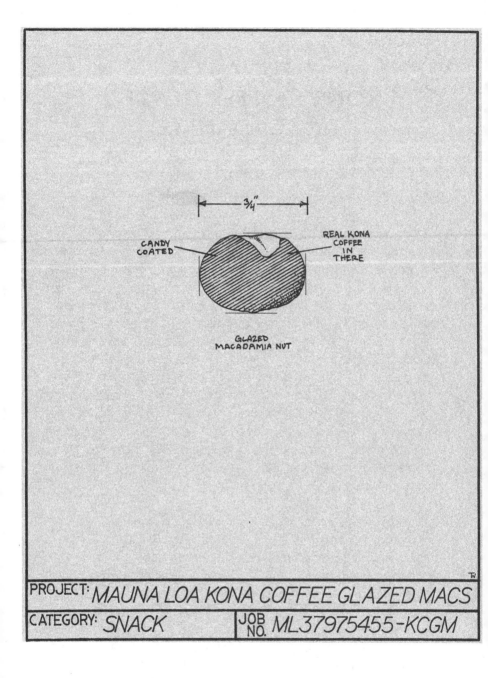

CANDY
COATED

REAL KONA
COFFEE
IN
THERE

¾"

GLAZED
MACADAMIA NUT

PROJECT: *MAUNA LOA KONA COFFEE GLAZED MACS*

CATEGORY: *SNACK*   JOB NO. *ML37975455-KCGM*

2. Combine the coffee, sugars, corn syrup, butter, and salt in a large saucepan and place over medium heat. Simmer the mixture and monitor it with a candy thermometer. Your target temperature is 290 degrees F, or just before the hard crack stage. The temperature continues to rise a bit after you turn off the heat, so you'll need to work quickly once you reach this target temp.

3. Lay a sheet of parchment paper on a baking sheet. This is where you will pour the coated nuts. You can also use a nonstick baking sheet for this or line the baking sheet with a silicone mat. When the candy is 290 degrees F, turn off the heat, and then stir in vanilla. Quickly stir in the hot macadamias until they are coated, then pour them out onto the parchment paper or nonstick pan. Separate the nuts as much as you can while they are still hot.

4. When the nuts have cooled, you can break them up into smaller, bite-size pieces. Store the nuts in a covered container in a dry spot.

• MAKES 4 CUPS.

• • • •

MCDONALD'S SWEET TEA

☆ ✌ 💣 ✏ ☯ ✂ ☞

I know, it's just tea. Tea and sugar, plain and simple—probably the easiest recipe on earth! But I have been getting so many requests to clone the sweet tea that McDonald's is heavily pitching these days for a buck a cup that I just can't ignore this product. Of course there are many ways to brew iced tea, but all you'll need to clone tea like Mickey D's are a few standard-size Lipton tea bags and a way to boil 2 quarts of water. There's a whole cup of sugar in there, so this tea is pretty sweet if you drink it straight. McDonald's serves the real stuff from a room-temperature jug into a cup filled with ice. This dilutes the tea so it's not so crazy-sweet when you take a big swig to wash down the nuggets.

2 quarts water
3 Lipton tea bags (standard size)

1 cup granulated sugar

1. Bring the water to a boil over high heat.
2. When the water hits a rolling boil, take it off the heat, add the tea bags, and cover the saucepan. Allow the tea to steep tea for 1 hour, and then remove the tea bags.
3. Add 1 cup of sugar to a 2-quart pitcher, then add the tea. Stir to dissolve the sugar. Pour the tea into a glass filled with ice to serve.

• MAKES 2 QUARTS.

• • • •

MCDONALD'S
VANILLA ICED COFFEE

☆   ✌   💣   ✏   ☯   ✂   ☞

In the coffee war that's been brewing since 2007, McDonald's is emerging victorious by snagging a significant chunk of the $11 billion coffee market away from sector-leader Starbucks. The hamburger chain's McCafe offerings, which include premium cappuccinos, lattes, and iced coffees, scored higher in taste tests according to *Consumer Reports* magazine, and the drinks come with a lower price tag than comparable beverages at the coffeehouse chain. The Vanilla Iced Coffee appears to be a standout selection at Mickey D's, and a home clone is simple after you get your hands on some Torani vanilla syrup. Brew up some coffee, chill it, and then pour these three ingredients over ice in a 16-ounce glass. The taste of your finished drink will be determined by the quality of your coffee (McDonald's has its own beans), so be sure to brew your favorite stuff. The better the coffee you start with, the better your clone will taste.

¹/₄ cup Torani vanilla syrup   *1 cup cold coffee*
¹/₄ cup half-and-half

1. Fill a 16-ounce cup with ice.
2. Pour the vanilla syrup over the ice, followed by the half-and-half and cold coffee. Serve with a straw.

• MAKES ONE 16-OUNCE SERVING.

Tidbits

You can find Torani vanilla syrup in many grocery stores, near the coffee, or at well-stocked liquor and bar supply stores.

* * *

MCDONALD'S CINNAMON MELTS

Everyone knows the center of a cinnamon roll is the best part. With that in mind, McDonald's designed a cinnamon pastry where every bite is coated with the same deliciously gooey cinnamon and brown sugar filling that you discover only after working your way through the dry, doughy part of traditional cinnamon rolls. It's sort of like monkey bread, whereby chunks of dough are tossed in cinnamon sugar and then baked in a deep cake pan. The difference with this clone of the McDonald's version is that the filling is mixed with margarine and spooned onto the dough chunks in layers. And you bake this in small, single-serving portions. As it turns out, a Texas-size muffin tin, which has cups that are about twice the size of a standard muffin tin, is the perfect pan for this. You can also use disposable aluminum pot pie pans that many markets carry. Since this recipe makes a dozen servings, dig this: After the cinnamon melts have cooled, cover and freeze them. When you need a quick breakfast pastry or late-night snack, simply remove a melt from the pan, microwave for 35 seconds or until hot (this is how McDonald's heats it, too), and you're instantly teleported to cinnamon roll paradise.

DOUGH

1 package active dry yeast
   (1/4 ounce)
1/2 cup warm water (105 to 110
   degrees F)
1/2 cup granulated sugar

1/2 cup whole milk
1/3 cup margarine, melted
2 eggs
1 teaspoon salt
4 cups all-purpose flour

FILLING

I cup packed dark brown sugar
2 tablespoons ground cinnamon

²/₃ cup margarine, melted

ICING

¹/₄ cup (¹/₂ stick) margarine,
   softened
¹/₂ cup (4 ounces) cream cheese,
   softened

I ¹/₂ cups powdered sugar
I tablespoon whole milk
¹/₂ teaspoon vanilla extract

1. To make the dough, dissolve the yeast in the warm water in a small bowl or measuring cup and let it sit for 5 minutes.

2. Use an electric mixer to combine the sugar with the milk and melted margarine in a large bowl. Mix in the eggs and salt. Mix in I cup of the flour. When the flour is combined, mix in I more cup of flour. Mix in the yeast solution, and then stir in the remaining 2 cups of flour with a wooden spoon. Use your hands to form the dough into a ball, and then put the dough back into the bowl, cover it, and store it in a warm place for about I¹/₂ hours.

3. Mix the filling ingredients together in a medium bowl, and then cover it until needed.

4. Roll the dough out on a floured surface until about ¹/₂ inch thick. Use a pizza slicer to slice the dough into approximately ¹/₂-inch-wide strips, and then slice those strips into ³/₄ -inch- to I-inch-long chunks of dough.

5. Use softened margarine to grease the cups of 2 large (Texas-size) 6-cup muffin tins. Drop 6 chunks of dough into the bottom of each cup. Spoon I to I¹/₂ teaspoons of cinnamon filling over the dough. Drop 7 more pieces of dough onto the filling in each cup, and then spoon 2 teaspoons of filling over the top of the dough. Cover the muffin tin with plastic wrap and let the dough sit in a warm spot for 30 minutes so that it rises a little more.

6. Preheat the oven to 350 degrees F.

7. Bake the cinnamon melts for I7 to 20 minutes, or until the dough turns light brown.

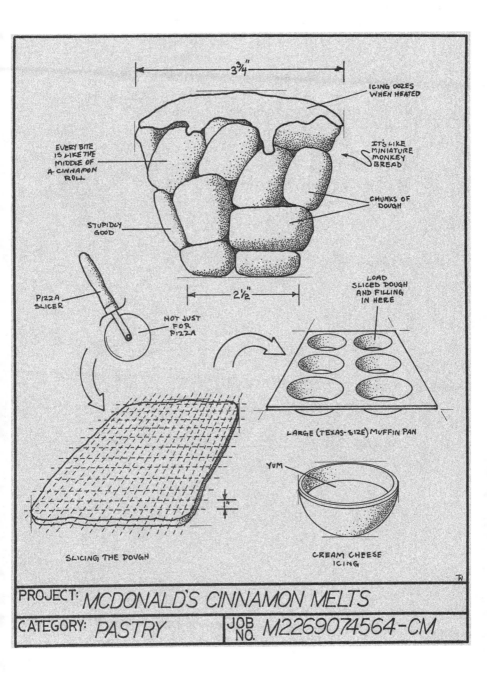

3¾"

ICING OOZES WHEN HEATED

EVERY BITE IS LIKE THE MIDDLE OF A CINNAMON ROLL

IT'S LIKE MINIATURE MONKEY BREAD

CHUNKS OF DOUGH

STUPIDLY GOOD

2½"

PIZZA SLICER

NOT JUST FOR PIZZA

LOAD SLICED DOUGH AND FILLING IN HERE

LARGE (TEXAS-SIZE) MUFFIN PAN

YUM

CREAM CHEESE ICING

SLICING THE DOUGH

½"

PROJECT: MCDONALD'S CINNAMON MELTS

CATEGORY: PASTRY

JOB NO. M2269074564-CM

8. As the cinnamon melts cool, make the icing by mixing the margarine and cream cheese together with an electric mixer on high speed. Add the powdered sugar and mix slowly until all the powdered sugar is incorporated. Add the milk and vanilla, then mix again on high speed until smooth and fluffy.

9. Spoon about 1 tablespoon of icing over the top of each cinnamon melt. Serve right away, or cool completely, then cover the melts with plastic and freeze. To prepare a frozen melt, remove one from the pan and microwave it on high for 35 to 45 seconds, or until warm.

• MAKES 1 DOZEN.

•   •   •   •

MCDONALD'S
FRUIT & WALNUT SALAD

☆　✌　🌑　✏　☯　✂　☞

McDonald's enlisted Destiny's Child, Venus Williams, and Bob Greene (Oprah's trainer) to kick off its balanced lifestyles campaign in the spring of 2005, starting with this salad and the tagline "Get a fruit buzz." Most of the recipe is no big secret: two kinds of sliced apples, red seedless grapes, and low-fat vanilla yogurt. But this new product did inspire another way to candy walnuts. It's a quick technique that includes honey and peanut oil, along with some granulated sugar and a little vanilla. Also, you should know that McDonald's has to use a special preservative coating on the apple slices to keep them from turning brown in the ten minutes or so that it takes for sliced apples to turn brown. Copy this recipe at home and you won't have to worry about such things.

CANDIED WALNUTS

1 teaspoon peanut oil	1/4 teaspoon vanilla extract
1 teaspoon honey	1/8 teaspoon salt
2 tablespoons granulated sugar	3/4 cup coarsely chopped walnuts

2 small Granny Smith apples, cored and cut into 16 slices each	40 red seedless grapes
	3/4 cup Dannon low-fat vanilla yogurt
2 small Gala apples, cored and cut into 16 slices each	

1. Make the candied walnuts by combining the peanut oil, honey, sugar, vanilla, and salt in a medium skillet over medium heat in

the order listed. When mixture begins to bubble, add the chopped walnuts and stir constantly until the sugar begins to smoke and/or caramelize. Immediately turn off the heat and keep stirring the nuts so that they do not burn. After a minute of stirring off the heat, pour the nuts out onto a plate. Toss the nuts as they cool so they don't stick together.

2. When the nuts have cooled, build each salad by mixing 8 slices of Granny Smith apple, 8 slices of Gala apple, 10 grapes, 3 tablespoons of yogurt, and 3 tablespoons of candied walnuts. Stir and serve.

- MAKES 4 SERVINGS.

•   •   •   •

MCDONALD'S
TANGY HONEY MUSTARD

☆　　✌　　💣　　✎　　☯　　✂　　☞

Certainly one of the tastiest dipping sauces that you can choose with your order of Chicken McNuggets is this sweet-and-sour creamy Dijon mustard. No longer shall you find it necessary to beg for extra packets of this sauce with your next box of cluck chunks. Now, with just four ingredients, you can from this day forward mix up the stuff at home anytime you want to use it as a spread on savory sandwiches (great with ham!) or as a dipping sauce for your own home-cooked nuggets or chicken strips.

5 tablespoons mayonnaise $1/2$ teaspoon white vinegar
2 tablespoons honey
4 teaspoons Grey Poupon
   Country Dijon Mustard

Combine all the ingredients in a small bowl. Cover and chill until needed.

• MAKES $1/2$ CUP.

·　　·　　·　　·

MCDONALD'S
MCLOBSTER SANDWICH

☆ ✌ 💣 ✏ ☯ ✂ ☞

On an excursion through Maine I saw an interesting sign advertising a lobster sandwich at the world's most famous hamburger chain. Lobster? I just had to get a closer look. When I got inside, a woman behind the counter told me that the sandwich is served only at select McDonald's locations, mostly in Maine, for a limited time only during the summer months. So I ordered one and sat down in the dining room to check it out. When I opened up the wrapper I found chilled fresh lobster chunks tossed in mayonnaise and piled on a hoagie roll with a leaf of lettuce—the McDonald's version of a lobster roll. I took a bite and it tasted pretty good. I ate the whole thing, ordered another one, and got back on the road. Driving off I thought about how strange it was to have been eating lobster at McDonald's. I also thought about how easy it would be to make a clone recipe for that sandwich and put it in this book.

½ cup cooked Maine lobster
   meat (chilled and chopped)
½ tablespoon mayonnaise

pinch salt
1 lettuce leaf
small hoagie roll

1. Mix together the chunks of lobster with the mayonnaise and salt.
2. Slice the hoagie roll lengthwise, and spread the lettuce leaf on the bottom half.
3. Spread the lobster over the lettuce. Top off the sandwich with the top half of the roll. Eat.

- MAKES 1 SANDWICH.

Tidbits
If you can't find fresh lobster, use canned Maine lobster.

•   •   •   •

MRS. FIELDS CRANBERRY WHITE CHOCOLATE COOKIES

☆   ✌   💣   ✏   ☯   ✂   ☞

Cranberries, white chocolate chips, walnuts, and rolled oats come together and party on in this re-creation of a cookie that's not only great for the holidays but will also turn the regular days into something special. As with any proper Mrs. Fields cookie clone, these cookies will, at first, seem underdone when they come out of the oven. But when the cookies cool down—as cookies will do—prepare to be tempted by a couple dozen sweet, circular masterpieces of taste bud joy with slightly crispy edges and soft, gooey centers.

1 cup (2 sticks) butter, softened	1 teaspoon baking soda
1 1/2 cups light brown sugar	3/4 teaspoon salt
1/4 cup granulated sugar	1/4 teaspoon ground cinnamon
2 eggs	1 1/2 cups chopped dried
1/4 teaspoons vanilla extract	cranberries
2 3/4 cups all-purpose flour	1 cup chopped walnuts
1 cup rolled oats (not instant)	3/4 cup white chocolate chunks
1 teaspoon baking powder	

1. Preheat the oven to 350 degrees F.
2. In a large bowl, cream together the butter, sugars, eggs, and vanilla with an electric mixer on high speed.
3. In another bowl, mix together the flour, oats, baking powder, baking soda, salt, and cinnamon.
4. Stir the dry ingredients into the wet stuff until blended. Stir in the cranberries, walnuts, and white chocolate.

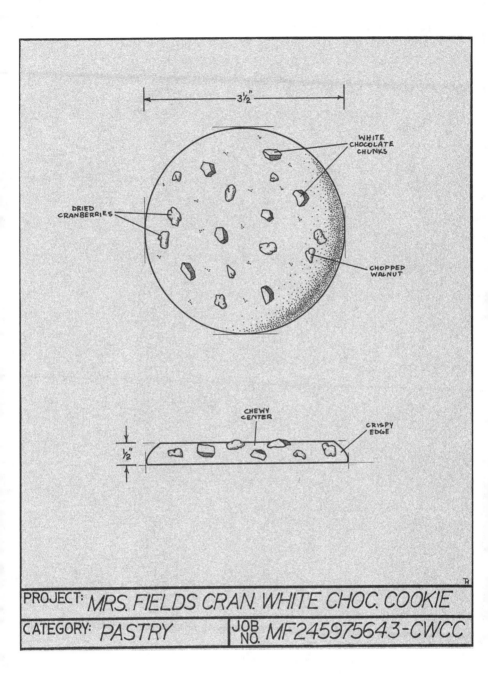

3½"

WHITE
CHOCOLATE
CHUNKS

DRIED
CRANBERRIES

CHOPPED
WALNUT

CHEWY
CENTER

CRISPY
EDGE

½"

PROJECT: MRS. FIELDS CRAN. WHITE CHOC. COOKIE

CATEGORY: PASTRY

JOB NO. MF245975643-CWCC

5. Spoon ¼ cup portions 2 inches apart onto a nonstick surface (parchment paper, silicone mat, or Release foil) on baking sheets. Bake for 15 to 18 minutes, or until the edges of the cookies are just beginning to brown—the cookies will still be soft in the center. Allow the cookies to cool for at least 15 minutes before serving.

• MAKES 2 DOZEN COOKIES.

• • • •

MRS. FIELDS
PUMPKIN HARVEST COOKIES

☆   ✌   🍒   ✏   ☯   ✂   ☞

You're not in the mood for pumpkin pie, but you want to bake something with pumpkin in it for the holidays? Give this clone of the seasonal Mrs. Fields favorite a shot. You'll use pure canned pumpkin; plus there are pecans in there and chunks of white chocolate that can be chopped up from bars. Nice! Pull the cookies out when they're still soft in the middle and just slightly browned around the edges, and you'll produce 2 dozen perfectly baked pumpkin-pumped happy pucks.

1 cup (2 sticks) butter, softened	1 teaspoon baking soda
2 cups packed dark brown sugar	1 1/4 teaspoons ground cinnamon
1 egg	3/4 teaspoon ground ginger
2 teaspoons vanilla extract	1/2 teaspoon ground nutmeg
3/4 cup canned pumpkin (pure pumpkin)	1/2 teaspoon ground allspice
2 1/2 cups all-purpose flour	12 ounces white chocolate chunks
1 teaspoon salt	1 1/2 cups chopped pecans
1 teaspoon baking powder	

1. Preheat the oven to 350 degrees F. In a large bowl, cream together the butter, sugar, egg, and vanilla with an electric mixer. Add the pumpkin and mix well.
2. In a separate bowl, stir together the flour, salt, baking powder, baking soda, and spices.
3. Combine the dry ingredients with the wet ingredients and mix well.

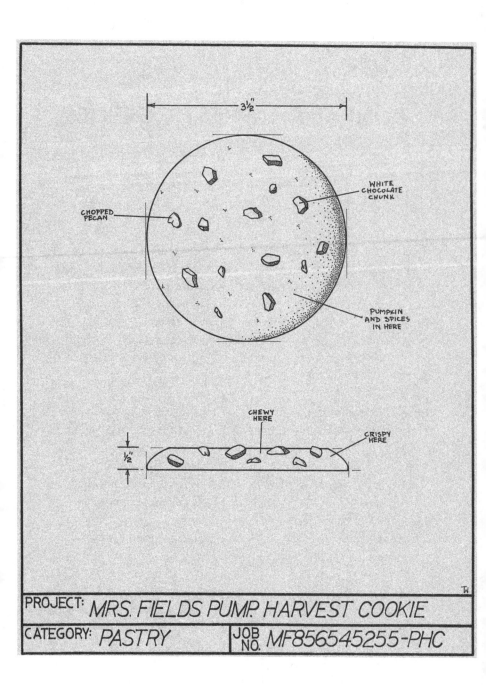

CHOPPED PECAN

WHITE CHOCOLATE CHUNK

PUMPKIN AND SPICES IN HERE

$3\frac{1}{2}"$

CHEWY HERE

CRISPY HERE

$\frac{1}{2}"$

TW

PROJECT: *MRS. FIELDS PUMP. HARVEST COOKIE*

CATEGORY: *PASTRY*   JOB NO. *MF856545255-PHC*

4. Add the white chocolate and pecans and stir until combined.

5. Measure ¼ cup portions 2 inches apart onto baking sheets that are lined with parchment paper or other nonstick material (such as a silicone mat or Release foil). Bake the cookies for 15 to 18 minutes, or until they are just beginning to brown slightly around the edges. The cookies will seem undercooked when they come out, but when cooled they will be crispy around the edges and soft in the center.

• MAKES 2 DOZEN COOKIES.

•   •   •   •

NO PUDGE!
ORIGINAL FAT FREE FUDGE
BROWNIE MIX

☆　　✌　　🌢　　✐　　☯　　✂　　☞

In 1995 pediatric nurse Lindsay Frucci discovered a way to make chewy, fudgy brownies without a smidgen of fat. Today you can find her pink brownie mix boxes in thousands of grocery stores and specialty markets throughout the country. All you have to do is add some nonfat vanilla yogurt to the dry mix and bake. The brownies that emerge from your oven are incredibly delicious, but the mix is on the expensive side. One box of No Pudge! Fat Free Fudge Brownie Mix will set you back around four bucks, which seems like a lot when you consider that boxes of regular brownie mix from larger brands such as Pillsbury or Duncan Hines contain similar ingredients but sell for roughly half that. So I spent a week burning through gobs of cocoa, sugar, and flour in hopes of discovering an easy way to re-create that tasty mix at a fraction of the cost of even the cheapest brownie mix on the market. After much trial and error I finally figured out how to do it! I tried many batches with Hershey's and Nestlé's cocoa but eventually decided the best widely available unsweetened cocoa powder for the task is the stuff made by Ghirardelli. Before you assemble this clone recipe, you'll also want to track down baker's sugar, which is a superfine sugar, and some powdered egg whites (health food stores or cake decorating suppliers carry this). Combine all the dry ingredients in a bowl, and when you're ready to make the brownies, simply mix in ⅔ cup of nonfat vanilla yogurt, just like with the real thing. In 34 baking minutes (same as regular minutes, but they seem much longer) you'll have one plate of amazing fat-free chocolate brownies

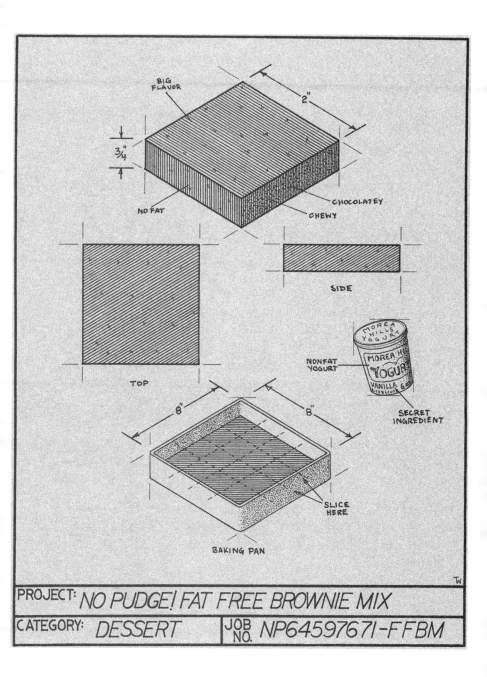

BIG FLAVOR

2"

3/4"

NO FAT

CHOCOLATEY

CHEWY

SIDE

TOP

NONFAT YOGURT

MOREA HILLS YOGURT

MOREA HILLS YOGUR

VANILLA 6 oz

SECRET INGREDIENT

8"

8"

SLICE HERE

BAKING PAN

ready to eat, and probably enough leftover ingredients to make another couple batches of mix that you can seal up and store for easy brownies anytime.

$^1/_3$ cup cake flour

2 tablespoons all-purpose flour

1 $^1/_4$ cups baker's sugar (superfine sugar)

$^1/_2$ cup Ghirardelli unsweetened cocoa powder

4 teaspoons powdered egg whites

1 tablespoon cornstarch

$^1/_2$ teaspoon salt

$^1/_4$ teaspoon baking soda

TO MAKE THE BROWNIES

$^2/_3$ cup nonfat vanilla yogurt

1. Combine all the ingredients in a medium bowl. Cover and store in a dry place until you're ready to make brownies.
2. To make the brownies, preheat your oven to 350 degrees F.
3. Spray an 8 x 8-inch metal baking pan with cooking spray.
4. Combine $^2/_3$ cup nonfat vanilla yogurt to the mix and blend with electric mixer for 1 minute, until the batter is smooth and shiny. Pour the batter into the pan and bake for 34 minutes. Cool and slice into squares.

• MAKES 16 BROWNIES.

Tidbits

The finished brownies freeze very well. Just slice the brownies and store them in a zip-top plastic freezer bag in your freezer. Thaw for 10 to 15 minutes before eating and they taste as good as when they were just baked!

•　•　•　•

NUTS 4 NUTS
CANDIED NUTS

☆   ✌   💣   ✏   ☯   ✂   ☞

The streets of New York City are peppered with Nuts 4 Nuts vendors selling freshly candied nuts that you can smell a block away. For a buck or two you get your choice of warm, sugar-coated almonds, peanuts, or cashews wrapped up in a little paper bag with the corners twisted closed. The nuts are candied right there on the carts in a large metal bowl over a heating element. When the nuts are added to sugar and water they are stirred vigorously until the water evaporates and the sugar crystallizes into a crunchy coating, without burning. They're easy to make on the street, which means they're even easier to clone at home. All you need for your own quick version of this addictive street snack is 1½ cups of your favorite raw nuts, some sugar, a little water, and a hot saucepan, and you're about 4 minutes away from an authentic New York City treat. The recipe works best in a pan that isn't nonstick, and the nuts must be raw. The oil added to roasted nuts prevents the sugar from properly crystallizing. Use this recipe with pecans or walnuts, and then sprinkle them over fresh spinach or baby greens, along with a little goat cheese or Gorgonzola and some diced apple or pear for an easy gourmet side salad.

2 tablespoons water   *1 ½ cups raw nuts (not roasted)*
¼ cup sugar

1. Bring the water and sugar to a boil in a medium saucepan over medium heat.
2. When the sugar has dissolved, add the nuts. Stir occasionally to coat the nuts. At about the 2-minute mark, stir vigorously. In

about a minute, the water will evaporate and the sugar will crystallize on the nuts. Turn off the heat immediately when all the sugar has crystallized on the nuts, but keep stirring. The sugar should begin to caramelize and turn light brown on the nuts. Pour the nuts onto a plate to cool.

- MAKES 1½ CUPS.

Tidbits

You can add other ingredients for flavor variations. Mix in ½ teaspoon ground cinnamon to the pan for cinnamon-flavored nuts. Add 1 teaspoon vanilla extract to the pan for vanilla nuts.

•   •   •   •

OLD BAY SEASONING

With spice grinder in hand, Gustav Brunn traveled to America from Germany and settled down in Baltimore on the Chesapeake Bay, where steamed crabs are a staple. Gustav began grinding. In 1939, after trying many different combinations, Gustav found just the right mix for a top-secret blend of spices that would be the most-used seasoning on steamed crabs, shrimp, lobster, and other tasty seafood dishes for generations to come. But McCormick & Co., which purchased Old Bay in 1990, insists that the celery salt–based blend is not just for seafood. You can also use the seasoning on chicken, french fries, popcorn, baked potatoes, deviled eggs, hamburgers, and even pizza.

1 tablespoon celery salt
1/4 teaspoon paprika
1/8 teaspoon ground black pepper
1/8 teaspoon cayenne pepper
pinch ground dry mustard
pinch ground mace

pinch ground cinnamon
pinch ground cardamom
pinch ground allspice
pinch ground cloves
pinch ground ginger

Combine all the ingredients in a small bowl. Store the seasoning in a sealed container.

- MAKES 4 TEASPOONS.

•   •   •   •   •

ORANGE JULIUS
BANANA JULIUS

This flavor variation from the Orange Julius company may be called Banana Julius, but they also add a little orange juice to the mix. Make sure your bananas are ripe for this clone so you get a nice sweet drink with the perfect thickness.

$^1/_2$ cup orange juice
3 tablespoons pasteurized egg white or egg substitute
1 teaspoon vanilla extract

$^1/_4$ cup sugar
2 medium ripe bananas
3 cups ice

1. Combine all the ingredients except the bananas and ice in a blender and blend on high speed for 15 seconds, or until the sugar is dissolved.
2. Add the bananas and ice and blend until the ice is crushed. Pour into two 16-ounce glasses, add a straw, and serve.

• MAKES 2 REGULAR-SIZE DRINKS.

• • • •

ORANGE JULIUS STRAWBERRY-BANANA CLASSIC SMOOTHIE

☆　　✌　　💣　　✏　　☯　　✂　　☞

As the trend for fruit smoothies surged in the 1990s, the Orange Julius company didn't want to be left out. After all, Orange Julius popularized the fruit smoothie with the original Orange Julius blended drink back in 1926. But as thicker smoothie drinks of more complex blends became popular, Orange Julius set out to put its own twist on the fruity beverage with a secret ingredient that is dumped into the blender along with the fruit, and a scoop of the original powdery compound that's added to the "Julius" drinks. This new powder, called coconut-almond compound, includes a frothing and thickening agent, plus a hint of coconut and almond flavorings. Now you can clone your own version of the most popular variety of the chain's Classic Smoothie using coconut syrup and almond extract as part of your own homemade secret recipe.

$1/2$ cup orange juice

3 tablespoons pasteurized egg white or egg substitute

1 teaspoon vanilla extract

$1/4$ cup sugar

$1/4$ cup milk

$1/4$ cup coconut syrup (such as Coco López)

$1/4$ teaspoon almond extract

2 medium ripe bananas

One 10-ounce box frozen strawberries in syrup, thawed

3 cups ice

1. Combine all the ingredients except the bananas, strawberries, and ice in a blender and blend on high speed for 15 seconds, or until the sugar is dissolved.
2. Add the banana, strawberries, and ice and blend until the ice is crushed. Pour into two 16-ounce glasses, add a straw, and serve.

• MAKES 2 REGULAR-SIZE DRINKS.

• • • •

PAL'S
SAUCE BURGER

☆   ✌   ●   ✎   ☯   ✂   ☞

Here's a simple, great-tasting burger from a small yet beloved Tennessee-based hamburger chain famous for its quirky buildings, tasty food, and "Sudden Service." Established in 1956 by Pal Barger, this twenty-one-unit fast-service chain accepted the Malcolm Baldrige National Quality Award from President George W. Bush and has performed admirably in markets among huge chains such as McDonald's, Burger King, and Wendy's. The signature sandwich from this little drive-thru comes slathered with a simple sauce—a combination of ketchup, mustard, and relish—that makes quick production of scores of these tasty burgers a breeze when the line of cars grows long, as it often does.

$1/8$ pound ground beef
1 small sesame seed bun
salt
2 tablespoons ketchup
1 teaspoon sweet pickle relish

$1/2$ teaspoon yellow mustard
1 drop hickory-flavored liquid
  smoke
pinch seasoned salt

1. Pat out the ground beef until it's about the same diameter as the bun. If you like, you can freeze this patty ahead of time to help keep the burger from falling apart when you cook it.
2. Brown or toast the faces of the top and bottom bun halves in a skillet or on a griddle over medium heat.
3. When the buns have browned, cook the hamburger patty in the hot pan or on the griddle. Lightly salt the meat.

4. Combine the ketchup, relish, mustard, liquid smoke, and seasoned salt in a small bowl.
5. When the meat is cooked, place the patty on the face of the bottom half of the bun.
6. Slather the sauce on the face of the top half of the bun, turn it over onto the meat, and dive in.

- MAKES 1 BURGER.

• • • •

PANERA BREAD
BROCCOLI CHEDDAR SOUP

☆   ✌   💣   ✏   ☯   ✂   ☞

The easy-melting, individually wrapped Kraft Cheddar Singles are the perfect secret ingredient for a home reconstruction of the delicious broccoli cheddar soup that's served at this top soup stop. In this clone, fresh broccoli is first steamed and then diced into little bits before combining with chicken broth, half-and-half, shredded carrot, and onion. Now you're just 30 minutes away from soupspoon go-time.

3 cups broccoli florets
4 cups chicken broth
1 cup half-and-half
$1/2$ cup all-purpose flour
8 slices Kraft Sharp Cheddar
   Singles

$1/2$ cup shredded carrot
$1/3$ cup diced white onion
pinch ground black pepper

1. Steam the broccoli on a steamer basket in a covered saucepan over boiling water for 6 minutes. Remove the broccoli to a chopping board, cool, then use a large sharp knife to dice the broccoli into pieces that are about the size of peas.
2. Pour the chicken broth into a large saucepan with the half-and-half. Whisk in the flour, and then add the remaining ingredients including the broccoli. Turn the heat to medium and cook, stirring often, until mixture begins to bubble. Reduce the heat and

simmer for 30 minutes, or until the carrots are tender and the soup is thick.

- MAKES 4 SERVINGS.

•   •   •   •

PANERA BREAD CRANBERRY WALNUT BAGEL

☆ ✌ 💣 ✏ ☯ ✂ ☞

I found that the best way to get the cranberry flavor and light pink color into this clone of the seasonal bagel from one of America's fastest-growing bread chains is to use concentrated cranberry juice found in the frozen food section of your market. First, thaw the juice, then shake the canister before you open it. After you've measured out the 3 tablespoons you'll need for this recipe, make the rest of the concentrate into juice and sip it with your freshly baked bagel clones. The most important step for commercial-quality chewy bagels is certainly no secret: a thorough kneading process. Make sure you knead the dough for at least 10 minutes to form a tough gluten framework. When you're forming your bagels and they start to stick to your fingers, add a little flour. It's okay if the bagels end up dusted with flour as they rise since any excess will wash off when boiling the bagels in the water solution. This final step before baking is called "kettling," and it is what gives bagels their shiny crust.

1 cup warm water
1 teaspoon active dry yeast
3 tablespoons cranberry juice cocktail frozen concentrate, thawed
1 tablespoon vegetable oil
2 1/2 cups bread flour (plus another 1/4 cup for kneading)

1/2 cup minced sweetened dried cranberries
1/3 cup finely chopped walnuts
1 teaspoon salt
4 quarts water
1/4 cup granulated sugar

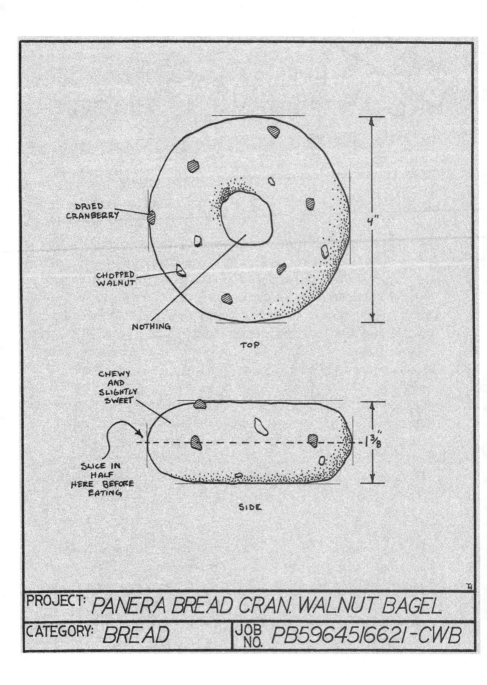

DRIED
CRANBERRY

CHOPPED
WALNUT

NOTHING

TOP

4"

CHEWY
AND
SLIGHTLY
SWEET

SLICE IN
HALF
HERE BEFORE
EATING

SIDE

$1\frac{3}{8}$"

PROJECT: PANERA BREAD CRAN. WALNUT BAGEL

CATEGORY: BREAD

JOB NO. PB59645I662I-CWB

1. Dissolve the yeast in the warm water in a large bowl. Make sure the water is warm, not hot, or you might kill the yeast. Add the cranberry juice concentrate and oil.

2. In another large bowl, combine the flour with the cranberries, walnuts, and salt.

3. Mix the flour into the yeast solution with a large spoon, and then use your hands to bring the dough together. Continue kneading, adding an additional ¼ cup of flour a little bit at a time when the dough gets tacky. Knead for 10 minutes, then form the dough into a ball and store it in a covered bowl for 30 minutes.

4. After the dough has rested divide it into 6 even portions. Form the bagels by rolling a portion of dough into a ball. Poke your thumbs through the middle of the dough ball, then stretch the dough out and spin it around your thumbs to create a doughnut shape. The hole should be about 1½ inches across. Place the formed dough onto a baking sheet rubbed with a little oil. Cover the dough (use an inverted baking sheet or dish towel) and set it in a warm spot for 30 minutes.

5. When the bagels have rested for the second time, preheat the oven to 400 degrees F.

6. Combine the water and sugar in a large saucepan or Dutch oven and place over high heat. When the water is boiling, drop the bagels into the water, 2 or 3 at a time, for 2 minutes. Use a slotted spoon or spider to flip the bagels after 1 minute. When you remove each bagel, let the excess water drip off, then place each on a baking sheet lined with parchment paper or Release foil. Bake the bagels for 28 to 32 minutes, or until browned.

• MAKES 6 BAGELS.

•   •   •   •

PANERA BREAD
FRENCH ONION SOUP

☆   ✌   💣   ✏   ☯   ✂   ☞

The 1,115 Panera Bread locations are famous for fantastic sandwiches, but it's this delicious French onion soup that has inspired the most e-mail requests for a clone from the chain. The biggest difference I find with Panera's formula versus other onion soup recipes is the inclusion of a small, almost undetectable, bit of tomato sauce. But rather than opening up a whole can of tomato sauce to use just 1 tablespoon in this home kitchen counterpart, I found that a squirt of ketchup works perfectly. Panera Bread also makes their soup with just a bit of heat, so we'll add a little Tabasco pepper sauce in the pot to wake everything up. The croutons on top of the soup appear to be made from the chain's focaccia that has been buttered, cubed, and toasted until crispy, but you can use any bread you may have on hand. As for the cheese on top, the menu says it's Asiago-Parmesan, but the cheese I tasted was more Asiago than Parmesan, so you'll need to use only Asiago cheese (that's been shaved using a potato peeler) for a great clone.

¼ cup butter
8 cups sliced white onions (4 to 5 medium onions)
two 14-ounce cans beef broth (I used Swanson)
¾ cup chicken broth (Swanson again)
3 tablespoons all-purpose flour
1½ cups water

1 tablespoon ketchup
1½ teaspoons ground black pepper
1½ teaspoons salt
¼ teaspoon dried thyme
¼ teaspoon garlic powder
couple drops Tabasco pepper sauce

GARNISH
croutons
shaved Asiago cheese

1. Melt the butter in a large saucepan over medium heat. Add the sliced onions and sauté for 15 to 20 minutes, stirring often, until the onions turn brown.
2. Add the remaining ingredients (but not the garnish) to the pan and stir to combine. Heat the soup until it's boiling, then reduce the heat and simmer uncovered for 20 minutes.
3. Make croutons for the top of the soup by slicing focaccia (or any bread you may have) into ¾-inch-thick slices. Butter both sides of those slices, then cut the slices into bite-size cubes. Bake the bread in a 425 degree F oven for 15 minutes, or until crispy. Shave some Asiago cheese by simply dragging a potato peeler over the edge of a wedge of Asiago.
4. Serve the soup super-hot after dropping in a handful of croutons, topped with a couple tablespoons of shaved Asiago cheese.

• MAKES EIGHT 1-CUP SERVINGS.

• • • •

PANERA BREAD
SPINACH ARTICHOKE BAKED EGG SOUFFLÉ

☆　　　✌　　　✲　　　✎　　　☯　　　✂　　　☞

Panera Bread's Baked Egg Soufflé reminds me of a breakfast Hot Pocket, if a Hot Pocket were to taste good. With eggs, cheese, spinach, and artichoke hearts baked into a buttery crust, this super-cool presentation will earn you big bonus points from your crew in the a.m. The best part is you won't have to stress out over making the dough from scratch since we use the premade Pillsbury Crescent Dough that comes in a tube. Just be sure that when you unroll the dough you don't separate it into triangles. Instead, you'll pinch the dough together along the diagonal perforations to make four squares. After the dough is rolled out, you can line four buttered ramekins with each square, and then fill each ramekin with the secret egg mixture and bake away. This recipe clones the spinach artichoke soufflé, but if you prefer the spinach and bacon version, check out the Tidbits below for that easy variation.

3 tablespoons thawed frozen
　　spinach
3 tablespoons minced artichoke
　　hearts
2 teaspoons minced onion
1 teaspoon minced red bell
　　pepper
5 eggs
2 tablespoons milk
2 tablespoons heavy cream

$1/4$ cup shredded cheddar cheese
$1/4$ cup shredded Monterey Jack
　　cheese
1 tablespoon shredded Parmesan
　　cheese
$1/4$ teaspoon salt
One 8-ounce tube Pillsbury
　　Crescent Butter Flake Dough
melted butter
$1/4$ cup shredded Asiago cheese

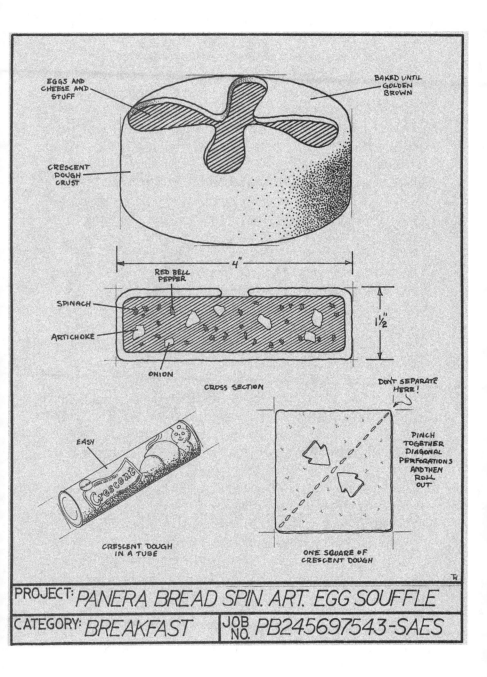

EGGS AND CHEESE AND STUFF

BAKED UNTIL GOLDEN BROWN

CRESCENT DOUGH CRUST

4"

RED BELL PEPPER

SPINACH

ARTICHOKE

1½"

ONION

CROSS SECTION

DON'T SEPARATE HERE!

EASY

Crescent

CRESCENT DOUGH IN A TUBE

PINCH TOGETHER DIAGONAL PERFORATIONS AND THEN ROLL OUT

ONE SQUARE OF CRESCENT DOUGH

PROJECT: *PANERA BREAD SPIN. ART. EGG SOUFFLE*

CATEGORY: *BREAKFAST*   **JOB NO.** *PB245697543-SAES*

1. Preheat the oven to 375 degrees F.
2. Combine the spinach, artichoke hearts, onion, and red bell pepper in a small bowl. Add 2 tablespoons water, cover the bowl with plastic wrap, and poke a few holes in the plastic. Microwave on high for 3 minutes.
3. Beat 4 of the eggs. Mix in the milk, cream, cheddar cheese, Jack cheese, Parmesan, and salt. Stir in the spinach, artichoke, onion, and bell pepper.
4. Microwave the egg mixture for 30 seconds on high, and then stir it. Do this 4 to 5 more times, or until you have a very runny scrambled egg mixture. This process will tighten up the eggs enough so that the dough won't sink into the eggs when it's folded over the top.
5. Unroll and separate the crescent dough into 4 portions. In other words, don't tear the dough along the perforations that make triangles. Instead, pinch the dough together along those diagonal perforations so that you have 4 rectangles of dough. Use some flour on the dough and roll across the width of each piece with a rolling pin so that the dough stretches out into a square that is approximately 6 inches by 6 inches.
6. Brush melted butter inside four 4-inch baking dishes or ramekins. Line each ramekin with the dough, then spoon equal amounts of egg mixture into each ramekin. Sprinkle 1 tablespoon of Asiago cheese on top of the egg mixture in each ramekin, and then gently fold the dough over the mixture.
7. Beat the last egg in a small bowl, then brush beaten egg over the top of the dough in each ramekin.
8. Bake for 25 to 30 minutes, or until the dough is lightly browned. Remove from the oven and cool for 5 minutes, then carefully remove the soufflés from each ramekin and serve hot.

- SERVES 4.

Tidbits

You can make the spinach and bacon version of this dish by substituting 4 pieces of cooked and crumbled bacon for the artichoke hearts. Simply leave the artichoke out of the recipe above, and then add the bacon to the egg mixture before you microwave it.

If you'd like to make bigger soufflés, double up on all the filling ingredients, and bake the soufflés in 6-inch ramekins. You will also have to extend the baking time by 5 minutes.

•   •   •   •

PEPPERIDGE FARM
SOFT BAKED
SNICKERDOODLE COOKIES

☆   ✌   💣   ✏   ☯   ✂   ☞

It's often the easiest recipes that yield the best food, and as far as cookies go, this simple clone reproduces one of my favorites. The cinnamon-and-sugar-topped snickerdoodles from Pepperidge Farm's line of soft cookies have a great taste and a perfect chewy consistency that makes eating just one an exercise in futility. The steps are pure Cookie Baking 101, but don't wander far from the kitchen when they bake. You have to be absolutely sure to yank these cookies out of the oven when they are just slightly browned and still soft. Then, after they cool, store the cookies in an airtight container to guarantee soft snickerdoodles for as long as the cookies last (which probably won't be too long).

½ cup (1 stick) butter, softened
½ cup granulated sugar
⅓ cup dark brown sugar
1 egg
1 teaspoon vanilla extract

1½ cups all-purpose flour
1 teaspoon baking soda
¼ teaspoon cream of tartar
¼ teaspoon salt

TOPPING
2 tablespoons granulated sugar   1 teaspoon ground cinnamon

1. Preheat the oven to 325 degrees F.
2. Using an electric mixer on medium speed, cream together the butter, sugars, egg, and vanilla in a medium bowl until smooth.

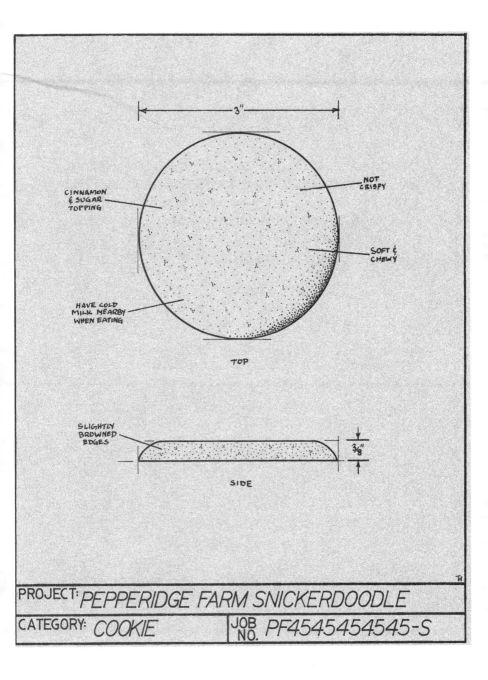

3"

CINNAMON
& SUGAR
TOPPING

NOT
CRISPY

SOFT &
CHEWY

HAVE COLD
MILK NEARBY
WHEN EATING

TOP

SLIGHTLY
BROWNED
EDGES

3/8"

SIDE

PROJECT: *PEPPERIDGE FARM SNICKERDOODLE*

CATEGORY: *COOKIE*

JOB NO. *PF4545454545-S*

153

3. In a separate bowl, stir together the flour, baking soda, cream of tartar, and salt.
4. Mix the dry ingredients into the wet stuff using the electric mixer on medium-low speed until the dough is smooth.
5. Mix the topping ingredients together in a small bowl.
6. Measure 1 heaping tablespoon of the dough and roll it into a ball with your hands.
7. Press the cookie dough ball into the cinnamon sugar. Place the ball, sugared side up, on a baking sheet lined with parchment paper. Bake for 14 to 16 minutes, or until the cookies just begin to turn light brown. Be careful not to bake the cookies too long, or they won't be soft like the originals.

- MAKES 16 COOKIES.

• • • •

POPEYES
BUTTERMILK BISCUITS

☆ ✌ ✊ ✎ ☻ ✂ ☞

In 2007 America's number one Cajun-style restaurant celebrated its 35th birthday with 1,583 stores worldwide. But Popeyes didn't start out with the name that most people associate with a certain spinach-eating cartoon character. When Al Copeland opened his first Southern-fried chicken stand in New Orleans in 1972, it was called Chicken on the Run. The name was later changed to Popeyes after Gene Hackman's character in the movie *The French Connection*. In addition to great spicy fried chicken, Popeyes serves up wonderful Southern-style buttermilk biscuits that we can now easily duplicate to serve with a variety of home-cooked meals. The secret is to cut cold butter into the mix with a pastry knife so that the biscuits turn out flaky and tender just like the originals.

2 cups all-purpose flour
1 tablespoon sugar
1 1/2 teaspoons salt
1 1/2 teaspoons baking powder

1/2 teaspoon baking soda
1/2 cup (1 stick) butter, cold
1/2 cup buttermilk
1/4 cup milk

TO BRUSH ON TOP
2 tablespoons butter, melted

1. Preheat the oven to 400 degrees F.
2. Mix together the flour, sugar, salt, baking powder, and baking soda in a medium bowl.

155

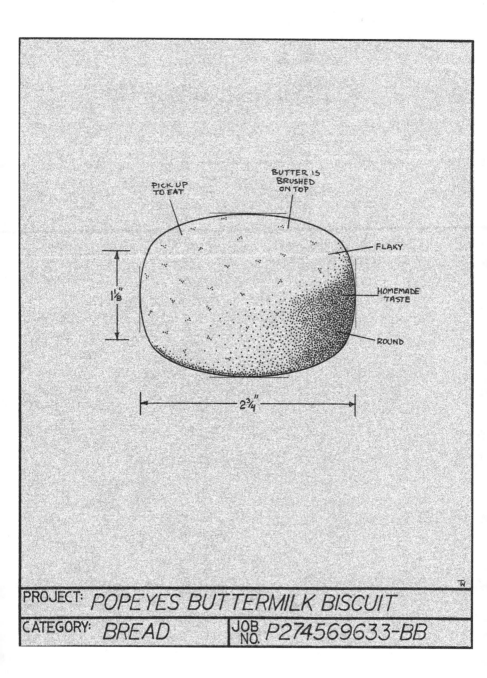

PICK UP
TO EAT

BUTTER IS
BRUSHED
ON TOP

FLAKY

HOMEMADE
TASTE

ROUND

1⅛"

2¾"

3. Slice the cold butter into cubes and use a pastry knife or potato masher to cut the butter into the dry mixture until no large chunks of butter remain.
4. Add the buttermilk and milk and stir with a spoon until a dough forms. Roll out to ½ inch thick on a floured surface.
5. Cut out biscuits with a 3-inch biscuit cutter and arrange on a lightly greased or parchment paper–lined baking sheet. Bake for 22 to 24 minutes, or until the tops begin to turn light brown. Remove the biscuits from the oven and cool for a couple of minutes, then brush each biscuit top with melted butter.

• MAKES 10 BISCUITS.

•　•　•　•

POPEYES CAJUN GRAVY

Ah, chicken gizzard. It took me more than eighteen years to find a recipe that requires chicken gizzard—not that I was looking for one. But I've seen the ingredients list on the box that comes from the supplier for the Cajun gravy from Popeyes, and if we're gonna do this one right I think there's got to be some gizzard in there. The gizzard is a small organ found in the lower stomach of a chicken, and your butcher should be able to get one for you. After you sauté and chop the gizzard, it is simmered with the other ingredients until you have a thick, authentic Southern gravy that goes great over the Popeyes Buttermilk Biscuits clone from page 155, or onto whatever begs to be swimming in pure flavor. Get ready for some of the best gravy that's ever come off your stovetop.

1 tablespoon vegetable oil
1 chicken gizzard
2 tablespoons minced green bell pepper
2½ ounces ground beef (¼ cup)
2½ ounces ground pork (¼ cup)
2 cups water
2 tablespoons cornstarch
1 tablespoon all-purpose flour
One 14-ounce can Swanson beef broth

2 teaspoons milk
2 teaspoons white vinegar
1 teaspoon sugar
1 teaspoon salt
⅛ teaspoon coarsely ground black pepper
¼ teaspoon cayenne pepper
⅛ teaspoon garlic powder
⅛ teaspoon onion powder
pinch dried parsley flakes

1. Heat the vegetable oil in a large saucepan over medium heat. Sauté the chicken gizzard in the oil for 4 to 5 minutes, until cooked. Remove the gizzard from the pan and let it cool so you can handle it. Finely mince the cooked gizzard.

2. Add the bell pepper to the saucepan and sauté it for 1 minute. Combine the ground beef and ground pork in a small bowl. Knead the meat together with your hands until it's well mixed. Add the ground beef and pork to the pan and cook it until it's browned. Use a potato masher to smash the meat into tiny rice-size pieces as it browns.

3. Whisk the cornstarch and flour into the water until there are no lumps, and then add the mixture to the saucepan. Stir.

4. Add the remaining ingredients and bring the mixture to a boil. Reduce the heat and simmer the gravy for 30 to 35 minutes, or until it's perfectly thick.

- MAKES 3 CUPS.

• • • •

POPEYES
CAJUN SPARKLE

☆　　✌　　💣　　✏　　☯　　✂　　☞

At these New Orleans–inspired quick-chicken restaurants portable paper pouches of this seasoning blend hold about ¼ teaspoon of tasty sprinkle, and Popeyes doesn't sell it in stores. The only way you'll get a decent portion to use on your home foods is to either horde dozens of envelopes of the Cajun seasoning or whip up your own home version. I recommend the latter. One secret ingredient in this basic seasoning blend is MSG, or monosodium glutamate, which is an important part of the delicious flavor. You'll find MSG near the other herbs and spices in your market under the brand-name Accent. If you don't want MSG on your food you can certainly leave this ingredient out of the mix. You won't get the best Top Secret clone, but the blend will still be very good on anything that needs a pinch of salt, flavor, and a little bit of spicy heat.

1 tablespoon salt
1/2 teaspoon ground black pepper
1/2 teaspoon garlic powder
1/2 teaspoon onion powder
1/2 teaspoon rubbed dried sage

1/4 teaspoon paprika
1/4 teaspoon MSG (such as Accent
    Flavor Enhancer)
1/8 teaspoon cayenne pepper

Combine all the ingredients in a small bowl. Sprinkle on stuff. Eat.

• MAKES 2 TABLESPOONS.

•　　•　　•　　•

POPEYES
RED BEANS & RICE (IMPROVED)

☆   ✌   💣   ✏   ☯   ✂   ☞

I first created the clone for this Cajun-style recipe back in 1994 for the second TSR book, *More Top Secret Recipes,* but I've never been absolutely pleased with the end result and vowed to one day rework it. After convincing a Popeyes manager to show me the ingredients written on the box of red bean mixture, I determined the only way to accurately clone this one is to include an important ingredient omitted from the first version: pork fat. Emeril Lagasse, a master of Cajun cooking, used to scream "pork fat rules" on his cooking show all the time, and in a dish like this one, he's right. One way to get the delicious smoky fat we need is to render it from smoked ham hocks, but that takes too long. The easiest way is to cook 4 or 5 pieces of bacon, save the cooked bacon for another recipe (or eat it!), and then use ¼ cup of the fat for this Top Secret clone. As for the beans, find red beans (they're smaller than kidney beans) in two 15-ounce cans. If you're having trouble tracking down red beans, red kidney beans will substitute nicely.

BEANS

¼ cup smoky pork fat (from
    cooking 4 to 5 slices of bacon)
two 15-ounce cans red beans
½ cup water

½ teaspoon brown sugar
⅛ teaspoon salt
pinch garlic powder
pinch onion powder

RICE

2¼ cups water
¼ cup (½ stick) butter

¼ teaspoon salt
1 cup converted rice

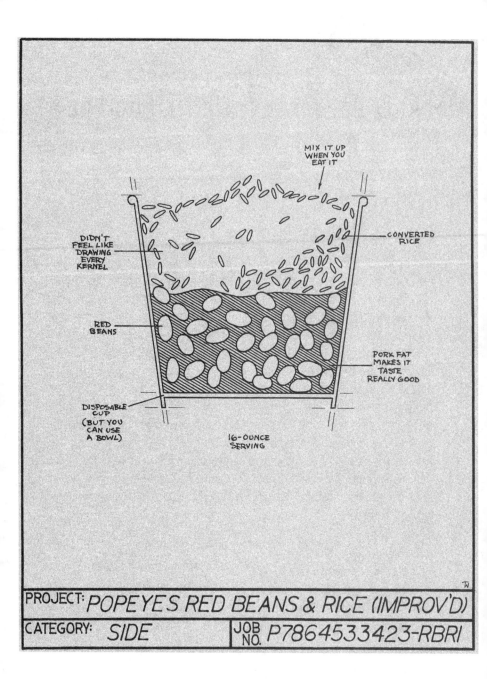

MIX IT UP
WHEN YOU
EAT IT

CONVERTED
RICE

DIDN'T
FEEL LIKE
DRAWING
EVERY
KERNEL

RED
BEANS

PORK FAT
MAKES IT
TASTE
REALLY GOOD

DISPOSABLE
CUP
(BUT YOU
CAN USE
A BOWL)

16-OUNCE
SERVING

TW

PROJECT: POPEYE'S RED BEANS & RICE (IMPROV'D)

CATEGORY: SIDE   JOB NO. P7864533423-RBRI

1. Combine the pork fat with one 15-ounce can red beans plus liquid in a medium saucepan. Add the water, brown sugar, salt, garlic powder, and onion powder. Bring the mixture to a boil, then reduce the heat and simmer for 20 minutes. Use a potato masher to smash the beans into a paste-like consistency. Add the entire contents of the remaining can of beans to the mixture and cook for an additional 10 minutes.
2. Prepare rice for 4 servings. For Uncle Ben's converted rice, you bring 2¼ cups water to a boil. Add ¼ cup butter and ¼ teaspoon salt. Add 1 cup rice, reduce the heat to low, and simmer for 20 minutes, or until tender.
3. To prepare each serving, scoop 1 cup of beans into a bowl. Add 1 cup of rice on top of the beans and serve.

• MAKES 2 LARGE SERVINGS.

• • • •

RAGÚ
PASTA SAUCES

☆ ✌ ✦ ✎ ◉ ✂ ☞

It's America's most popular pasta sauce, and now you can whip up clones of two varieties at home at a fraction of the cost. Just snag a large can of tomato sauce and a few other common ingredients and get on with the simmering. These recipes duplicate the traditional "Meat" variety of the sauce and the newer "Chunky Garden Style" version with tomato, basil, and Italian cheese. Feel free to doctor these sauces up with your own creative additions (sliced mushrooms, fresh garlic, etc.) just as you may do to perk up real Ragú.

MEAT

2 ounces ground beef
one 29-ounce can tomato sauce
5 teaspoons granulated sugar
4 teaspoons olive oil
1 ½ teaspoons minced dried onions

1 ½ teaspoons shredded Romano cheese
⅛ teaspoon ground black pepper
1 bay leaf

TOMATO, BASIL, AND ITALIAN CHEESE

one 29-ounce can tomato sauce
½ cup canned diced tomatoes
5 teaspoons granulated sugar
1 tablespoon olive oil
1 tablespoon shredded Romano cheese
1 teaspoon shredded Parmesan cheese

1 teaspoon dried basil
½ teaspoon dried parsley
¼ teaspoon garlic powder
⅛ teaspoon black pepper
1 bay leaf

MEAT

Brown the ground beef in a medium saucepan over medium heat. Add the remaining ingredients, bring to a boil, then reduce the heat and simmer for 15 to 20 minutes, stirring often.

*   MAKES 2½ CUPS.

TOMATO, BASIL & ITALIAN CHEESE

Combine all the ingredients in a medium saucepan and place over medium heat. Bring to a boil, then reduce the heat and simmer for 15 to 20 minutes, stirring often.

*   MAKES 3 CUPS.

• • • •

RONDELÉ
GARLIC & HERBS CHEESE
SPREAD

☆ ✌ 🔥 ✏ ☯ ✂ ☞

The real thing found in the deli section of your market is used on crackers, as a dip for raw vegetables, or even as a spread on sandwiches, burgers, and wraps. Now I've come up with an easy way to duplicate Rondelé using a 12-ounce tub of whipped cream cheese—which means you'll happily get three times the amount of the 4-ounce original! Just be sure when mixing your version that you don't overmix, or you will destroy the fluffiness of the whipped cheese. The Italian seasoning included here is a dried herb blend (usually marjoram, thyme, rosemary, savory, sage, oregano, and basil) found near the other bottled herbs and spices in your market. I used McCormick brand for this clone, but any brand should work fine. Since the herbs are dried, the flavor is more subtle than it would be with fresh herbs, even after the dried bits soak up moisture from the cheese. And that's just want we want for a proper clone.

one 12-ounce tub Philadelphia
  whipped cream cheese
1 ½ teaspoons finely minced fresh
  garlic
¾ teaspoon Italian seasoning

¼ teaspoon plus ⅛ teaspoon
  salt
⅛ teaspoon onion powder

Gently stir the garlic, Italian seasoning, salt, and onion powder into the whipped cream cheese. Store the spread in your fridge for at least a couple of hours. Overnight is even better. Stir once more before serving.

- MAKES 12 OUNCES.

•   •   •   •

SABRA
CLASSIC HUMMUS

☆　　　✌　　　💣　　　✎　　　🎱　　　✂　　　☞

Every brand of hummus I've tried over the years has been just average in taste and texture, until I discovered Sabra. Now this ultra-smooth hummus—which has been rated number one in a blind taste test, according to Sabra's Web site—is the only hummus in my fridge, unless I've made this clone. Hummus is an awesome snack as a dip for vegetables or pita chips, since it's rich in protein, soluble fiber, potassium, and vitamin E. The secret to duplicating Sabra's smooth and creamy quality is to let your food processor work the stuff over for a solid 10 minutes. Also, don't use all the liquid from the can of garbanzo beans or the hummus will end up too runny. Strain off the liquid first, then measure only ½ cup back into the food processor. Sabra uses canola and/or soybean oil, but you may think olive oil tastes even better. Look for a jar of sesame tahini in the aisle where all the international foods are parked, and while you're there find the citric acid, which may also go by the name "sour salt." The clone below will not have the proper tang without this secret ingredient, and citric acid also works as a preservative to help the leftover hummus stay fresh and tasty.

one 16-ounce can garbanzo
  beans (chickpeas), strained
½ cup liquid from garbanzo
  beans
3 tablespoons sesame tahini
  (sesame seed paste)
3 tablespoons canola oil (or olive
  oil)

1 teaspoon lemon juice
½ teaspoon finely minced garlic
¼ teaspoon plus ⅛ teaspoon salt
¼ teaspoon plus ⅛ teaspoon
  citric acid (sour salt)
¼ teaspoon ground white pepper

1. Pour the canned garbanzo beans into a strainer over a bowl to catch the liquid.
2. Combine the strained garbanzo beans, the ½ cup liquid (toss out the rest), and the remaining ingredients in a food processor. Process on high speed for 10 minutes. Store the hummus in a covered container in your refrigerator until chilled.

- MAKES 14 OUNCES.

• • • •

SKYLINE
CHILI

☆   ✌   🍖   ✏   ☯   ✂   ☞

Nope, there's no chocolate in it. Or coffee. Or Coca-Cola. The ingredient rumors for Skyline Chili are plentiful on the Internet, but anyone can purchase cans of Skyline chili from the company and find the ingredients listed right on the label: beef, water, tomato paste, dried torula yeast, salt, spices, cornstarch, and natural flavors. You can trust that if chocolate were included in the secret recipe, the label would reflect it—important information for people with a chocolate allergy. All it takes to re-create the unique flavor of Skyline is a special blend of easy-to-find spices plus beef broth and a few other not-so-unusual ingredients. Let the chili simmer for an hour or so, then serve it up on its own or in one of the traditional Cincinnati-style serving suggestions (the "ways" they call 'em) with the chili poured over spaghetti noodles, topped with grated cheddar cheese and other good stuff:

3-WAY
Pour chili over cooked spaghetti noodles and top with grated cheddar cheese.

4-WAY
Add a couple teaspoons of grated onion before adding the cheese.

5-WAY
Add cooked red beans over the onions before adding the cheese.

1 pound ground beef
1/2 cup water
2 tablespoons cornstarch
two 14.5-ounce cans Swanson
   beef broth
one 6-ounce can tomato paste
4 teaspoons chili powder
1 tablespoon white vinegar

1 1/4 teaspoons salt
1 teaspoon ground cardamom
1 teaspoon ground nutmeg
1/4 teaspoon ground allspice
1/4 teaspoon cayenne pepper
1/4 teaspoon ground coriander
1/4 teaspoon garlic powder
1/8 teaspoon ground black pepper

1. Brown the ground beef in a large saucepan over medium heat. Do not drain. Use a potato masher to mash the ground beef into very small pieces that are about the size of rice.
2. Dissolve the cornstarch in the water, and then add the solution (slurry) plus the remaining ingredients to the pan. Bring the mixture to a boil, then reduce the heat and simmer for 60 to 75 minutes, or until thick.

• MAKES 5 CUPS.

• • • •

SONIC DRIVE-IN
PEANUT BUTTER SHAKE AND
PEANUT BUTTER FUDGE SHAKE

☆　　✌　　💣　　✏　　☯　　✂　　☞

These easy-to-make milkshake clones from Sonic's fountain are no longer available at the 3,342-unit drive-in burger chain, but you'll always have this clone. The straight peanut butter version is way delicious if you're into peanut butter. And then, when you add a little fudge to the recipe for the second clone, you've got what tastes like a cold, creamy Reese's Peanut Butter Cup. Good stuff, man.

PEANUT BUTTER SHAKE

2 1/4 cups vanilla ice cream
1/4 cup whole milk

2 tablespoons creamy peanut butter

PEANUT BUTTER FUDGE SHAKE

2 1/4 cups vanilla ice cream
1/4 cup whole milk

2 tablespoons creamy peanut butter
1 tablespoon chocolate fudge

1. Combine the ingredients for the shake of your choice in a blender. Be sure to pack the ice cream into the measuring cup when you measure it out. Blend everything on medium speed until smooth.
2. Pour the shake into a 16-ounce glass, add a straw, and serve it up. Pop the shake into the freezer for 10 to 15 minutes to firm it up if it's too runny.

• MAKES 1 SERVING.

SONIC DRIVE-IN
STRAWBERRY CHEESECAKE
SHAKE

The cool thing about this Top Secret Recipe is that many of the ingredients come in a kit designed for making strawberry cheesecake. Find Jell-O No Bake Strawberry Cheesecake Mix near the puddings in your supermarket and you have half the ingredients locked up. Inside the box are three separate packets: strawberries in syrup, the cheesecake mix powder, and graham cracker crumbs. You'll also need vanilla ice cream, a cup of milk, and a little whipped cream. Toss the first four ingredients below in a blender until smooth, fill 2 glasses, and then top off the shakes with whipped cream and graham cracker crumbs from the kit. Now get ready, because everyone is about to freak out when they suck strawberry cheesecake through a straw! The recipe below makes 2 regular-size shakes, but you can make another 2 shakes using up the remaining strawberries from the cheesecake kit. If you get some additional strawberries in syrup from the frozen food aisle in your market, you can make as many as 8 more shake clones with the remaining cheesecake mix powder and graham cracker crumbs.

1 cup milk

3 cups vanilla ice cream

½ cup strawberries and syrup (from Jello-O No Bake Strawberry Cheesecake kit)

3 tablespoons cheesecake mix powder (from cheesecake kit)

ON TOP

canned whipped cream

2 teaspoons graham cracker crumbs (from cheesecake kit)

1. Combine the milk, ice cream, strawberries, and cheesecake mix in a blender and mix on high speed until smooth. Pour into two 12-ounce glasses.
2. Garnish the top with a squirt of whipped cream from a can and about a teaspoon of graham cracker crumbs from the cheese-cake kit. Serve each shake with a straw.

- MAKES 2 REGULAR-SIZE DRINKS.

• • • •

SONIC DRIVE-IN
SONIC BURGER

☆   ✌   🔥   ✏   ☯   ✂   ☞

Driving through Louisiana in 1953, Troy Smith discovered a hamburger stand that had installed an intercom system to speed up ordering. Troy thought the idea of ordering food from parked cars would be perfect for his Top Hat Restaurant in Stillwater, Oklahoma. He borrowed a bunch of cars from a friend who owned a used car lot and parked the cars in a row as a guide to form stalls around his restaurant. He wired an intercom system to the stalls and renamed his drive-in "Sonic" with the slogan "Service with the Speed of Sound." The new concept was a smash, and revenues for the redesigned hot dog and hamburger stand doubled during the first week. There are no secret ingredients in this clone of Sonic's signature hamburger— just common hamburger components. It's all in how you stack the ingredients that makes this burger taste like a Sonic Burger.

$1/4$ pound ground beef
1 large plain white hamburger
   bun
butter-flavored spray or melted
   butter
salt
ground black pepper

2 teaspoons mayonnaise
3 dill pickle slices (hamburger
   slices)
1 tablespoon chopped white
   onion
$1/3$ cup chopped iceberg lettuce
2 tomato slices

1. Shape the ground beef into a patty with approximately the same diameter as the bun. Cover the patty with wax paper and freeze it.

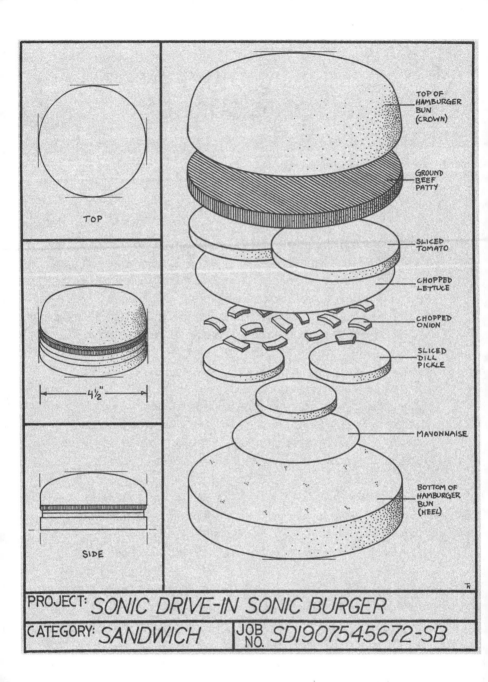

TOP

TOP OF
HAMBURGER
BUN
(CROWN)

GROUND
BEEF
PATTY

SLICED
TOMATO

CHOPPED
LETTUCE

CHOPPED
ONION

SLICED
DILL
PICKLE

MAYONNAISE

BOTTOM OF
HAMBURGER
BUN
(HEEL)

4½"

SIDE

PROJECT: *SONIC DRIVE-IN SONIC BURGER*

CATEGORY: *SANDWICH*   **JOB NO.** *SDI907545672-SB*

2. When you're ready to prepare the burger, preheat a large skillet or griddle over medium heat.
3. Spray some butter spray or spread a thin layer of melted butter on the top and bottom bun halves. Lightly brown the bun in the skillet or on the griddle, then set it aside.
4. Cook the beef patty in the hot pan, and lightly season it with salt and pepper. Cook the beef for 3 to 4 minutes per side, until done.
5. As the patty cooks, start building the burger by first spreading the mayonnaise over the browned face of the bottom bun.
6. Arrange the pickle slices on the mayonnaise.
7. Sprinkle the chopped onion over the pickles.
8. Arrange the lettuce on the onions.
9. Stack the tomato slices on the lettuce.
10. When the beef is done, stack it on the lettuce, and then top off the sandwich with the top bun. You may want to pop the burger in your microwave on high for 10 to 15 seconds. This will warm the bread, as if the sandwich had been wrapped up in paper as they do at the chain.

• MAKES 1 SANDWICH.

•   •   •   •

SONIC DRIVE-IN HICKORY BURGER

☆   ✌   💣   ✐   ☯   ✂   ☞

Word quickly spread through Oklahoma of Sonic's early success in the 1950s. One day Sonic Drive-In founder Troy Smith noticed a man measuring car stalls that surrounded the restaurant. Troy went to see what was going on, and the man introduced himself as Charles Woodrow Pappe, an entrepreneur. Charles said that he was trying to figure out why the stalls were different sizes and if this had something to do with the booming business at the restaurant. Troy explained that he lined up several cars from his friend's used car lot to lay out the stalls and that the varying stall sizes were not part of the business plan—the cars he used were different sizes. The two men hit it off after that, and Charles eventually became the first franchise owner of a Sonic Drive-In, in Woodward, Oklahoma, in 1956. This burger variation is similar to the Sonic Burger, but with smoky BBQ sauce instead of mayo, and no pickles or sliced tomato.

¹/₄ pound ground beef	ground black pepper
1 large plain white hamburger bun	1 tablespoon Kraft Hickory BBQ Sauce
butter-flavored spray or melted butter	1 tablespoon chopped white onion
salt	¹/₃ cup chopped iceberg lettuce

1. Shape the ground beef into a patty with approximately the same diameter as the bun. Cover the patty with wax paper and freeze it.

2. When you're ready to prepare the burger, preheat a large skillet or griddle over medium heat.

3. Spray some butter spray or spread a thin layer of melted butter on the top and bottom bun halves. Lightly brown the bun in the skillet or on the griddle, then set it aside.

4. Cook the beef patty in the hot pan, and lightly season it with salt and pepper. Cook the beef for 3 to 4 minutes per side, until done.

5. As the patty cooks, build the burger by first spreading the BBQ sauce on the bottom bun half.

6. Sprinkle the chopped onion over the sauce.

7. Arrange the lettuce on the onion.

8. When the beef is done, stack it on the lettuce, and then top off the sandwich with the top bun half. Pop the burger in your microwave on high for 10 to 15 seconds to warm the bread, as if the sandwich had been wrapped up in paper as they serve it at the chain.

- MAKES 1 SANDWICH.

• • • •

SONIC DRIVE-IN
JALAPEÑO BURGER

☆   ✌   💣   ✏   ☯   ✂   ☞

By 1978 there were more than 800 Sonic Drive-Ins in 13 states, but throughout the 1960s and 1970s there were no standardized procedures in place for franchisees. Recipes varied from restaurant to restaurant, so loyal customers never really knew what their burger would taste like when visiting a new location. This inconsistency caused a sharp decline in business, and by the 1980s Sonic was in trouble. A new management team came on board in the mid-'80s and established standard franchise procedures and a Sonic Management School that turned the company around. Sonic later redesigned all stores with a "retro-future" look, and today business is booming. These days a jalapeño burger that you purchase in Seattle, Washington, is guaranteed to look and taste the same as one purchased near Sonic's headquarters in Oklahoma City. How many jalapeño slices can you handle on your burger? Now you can find out.

¼ pound ground beef
1 large plain white hamburger
   bun
butter-flavored spray or melted
   butter
salt

ground black pepper
1½ teaspoons yellow mustard
6 to 10 bottled jalapeño slices
   (nacho slices)
⅓ cup chopped lettuce

1. Shape the ground beef into a patty with approximately the same diameter as the bun. Cover the patty with wax paper and freeze it.

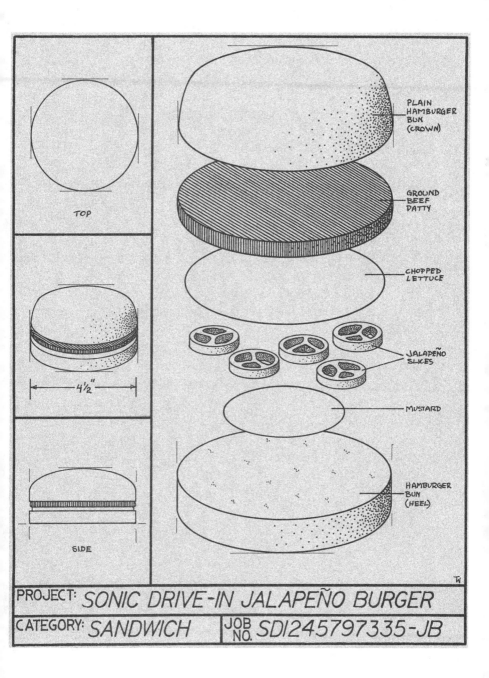

TOP

4½"

SIDE

PLAIN
HAMBURGER
BUN
(CROWN)

GROUND
BEEF
PATTY

CHOPPED
LETTUCE

JALAPEÑO
SLICES

MUSTARD

HAMBURGER
BUN
(HEEL)

TW

PROJECT: *SONIC DRIVE-IN JALAPEÑO BURGER*

CATEGORY: *SANDWICH*   JOB NO. *SDI245797335-JB*

2. When you're ready to prepare the burger, preheat a large skillet or griddle over medium heat.
3. Spray some butter spray or spread a thin layer of melted butter on the top and bottom bun halves. Lightly brown the bun in the skillet or on the griddle, then set it aside.
4. Cook the beef patty in the hot pan, and lightly season it with salt and pepper. Cook the beef for 3 to 4 minutes per side, until done.
5. As the patty cooks, build the burger by first spreading mustard over the face of the bottom bun.
6. Arrange the jalapeño slices on the mustard.
7. Arrange the lettuce on the jalapeño slices.
8. When the beef is done, stack it on the lettuce, and then top off the sandwich with the top bun half. Warm the bun by popping the burger in your microwave on high for 10 to 15 seconds. This will make the sandwich feel like it was wrapped in paper straight off the assembly line.

• MAKES 1 SANDWICH.

• • • •

THE SOUP NAZI'S CRAB BISQUE

☆ ✌ 💣 ✏ ☯ ✂ ☞

New Yorkers would line up around the block at the 55th Street location to get a hot cup of Al Yeganeh's delicious soup at Soup Kitchen International. And everyone was familiar with the demands posted near the order window: "Pick the soup you want!" "Have your money ready!" and "Move to the extreme left after ordering!" Violate any of these rules and Al sent you to the back of the line, even if you had waited for as long as two hours to get to the front. this is precisely how Yeganeh was portrayed by actor Larry Thomas in *Seinfeld* episode number 116, when he forever became known as the Soup Nazi. After that episode aired a new rule was posted: "Do not mention the N Word (Nazi)! In 2006 the original location closed and Al went into the business of franchising his concept under the new name "the Original SoupMan." Today there are more than fifty franchises throughout the United States and Canada, including six in Manhattan. But the recipes are still a secret, even from franchisees, since the soups are delivered premade to each location in 8-pound bags. Among the favorites to this day is the crab bisque, which is the soup Jerry orders on the show.

4 pounds snow crab legs
4 quarts water (16 cups)
1 small onion, chopped
1 ½ stalks celery, chopped
2 cloves garlic, quartered
2 potatoes, peeled and chopped
¼ cup butter

¼ cup chopped fresh Italian parsley
⅓ cup tomato sauce
¼ cup heavy cream
1 tablespoon chopped pimento
½ teaspoon coarsely ground black pepper

¹/₄ teaspoon dried thyme
¹/₄ teaspoon dried basil

¹/₄ teaspoon dried marjoram
2 bay leaves

1. Remove all the crab meat from the shells and set the meat aside.
2. Put half the shells into a large pot with the water and place over high heat. Add the onion, 1 stalk of chopped celery, and the garlic, then bring the mixture to a boil. Reduce heat and simmer for 1 hour, stirring occasionally (the white part of the shells will start to become transparent), then strain the stock. Discard the shells, onion, celery, and garlic, keeping only the stock.
3. Measure 3 quarts (12 cups) of the stock into a large saucepan or cooking pot. If you don't have enough stock, add enough water to make 3 quarts.
4. Add the potatoes, bring the mixture to a boil, then add half the crab and the remaining ingredients to the pot and bring it back to boiling. Reduce the heat and simmer uncovered for 2 hours, until it thickens. Add the remaining crab and simmer for another hour or so, until the soup is very thick.

• MAKES 4 TO 6 SERVINGS.

•   •   •   •

THE SOUP NAZI'S
CREAM OF SWEET POTATO
SOUP

☆　　✌　　💣　　✎　　🎱　　✂　　☞

After the "Soup Nazi" episode of *Seinfeld* aired, Jerry Seinfeld and several members of his production crew went over to Soup Kitchen International in New York City for lunch. When owner Al Yeganeh recognized Jerry he flew into a profanity-filled rant about how the show had "ruined" his business and he demanded an apology. According to writer Spike Feresten, Jerry gave "the most insincere, sarcastic apology ever given," Yeganeh yelled, "No soup for you!" and immediately ejected them from the premises. Knowing that to upset Al was to risk being yelled at and possibly evicted like Jerry, it was with great caution that I approached the order window to ask the Soup Nazi a few questions about the November 1995 *Seinfeld* episode that made him famous. Needless to say, the interview was very brief.

> **TW:** How do you feel about all the publicity that followed the *Seinfeld* episode?
> **AY:** I didn't need it. I was known well enough before that. I don't need it.
> **TW:** But it must have been good for business, right?
> **AY:** He [Seinfeld] used me. He used me. I didn't use him, he used me.
> **TW:** How many people do you serve in a day?
> **AY:** I cannot talk to you. If I talk I cannot work.
> **TW:** How many different soups do you serve?
> **AY:** (Getting very upset) I cannot talk! (Pointing to sign) Move to the left! Next!

4 sweet potatoes (about I pound each)
4 cups low-sodium chicken broth
4 cups water
I cup roasted cashews
$\frac{1}{3}$ cup butter

$\frac{1}{2}$ cup tomato sauce
2 tablespoons heavy cream
2 teaspoons salt
$\frac{1}{8}$ teaspoon ground black pepper
pinch dried thyme

1. Preheat the oven to 400 degrees F. Bake the sweet potatoes for 45 to 60 minutes, or until they are soft. Cool the potatoes until they can be handled.

2. Peel away the skin, then put the potatoes into a large bowl. Mash the potatoes for 15 to 20 seconds, until just a few chunks remain.

3. Spoon the mashed sweet potatoes into a large saucepan, add the remaining ingredients, stir to combine, and set the heat to medium.

4. When the soup begins to boil, reduce the heat and simmer for 50 to 60 minutes. The cashews should be soft. Serve hot with an attitude.

• MAKES 6 TO 8 SERVINGS.

•   •   •   •

THE SOUP NAZI'S
INDIAN MULLIGATAWNY

☆　　✌　　💣　　✏　　☯　　✄　　☞

Elaine: "Do you need anything?"
Kramer: "Oh, a hot bowl of Mulligatawny would hit the spot."
Elaine: "Mulligatawny?"
Kramer: "Yeah, it's an Indian soup. Simmered to perfection by one of the great soup artisans in the modern era."
Elaine: "Oh. Who, the Soup Nazi?"
Kramer: "He's not a Nazi. He just happens to be a little eccentric. You know, most geniuses are."

Kramer was right. Al Yeganeh—otherwise known as the Soup Nazi from the Seinfeld episode that aired in 1995—is a master at the soup kettle. His popular soup creations have inspired many inferior copycats in the Big Apple, including the Soup Nutsy, which was only ten blocks away from Al's original location on 55th Street. Yeganeh's mastery shows when he combines unusual ingredients to create unique and delicious flavors in his much-raved-about soups. In this one, you might be surprised to discover pistachios and cashews among the many vegetables. But it's a combination that works.

I took a trip to New York and tasted about a dozen of the Soup Nazi's original creations. This one, the Indian Mulligatawny, was high on my list of favorites. After each daily trip to Soup Nazi headquarters (Soup Kitchen International), I immediately headed back to the hotel and poured samples of the soups into labeled, sealed containers, which were then chilled for the trip back home. Back in the underground lab, portions of the soup were rinsed through a sieve so that ingredients could be identified. I re-created four of Al's bestselling soups after that trip, including this one, which will need to simmer for 3 to 4 hours, or until the soup reduces. The soup will darken as the flavors intensify, the potatoes will begin to fall apart to thicken the soup, and the nuts will soften. If you follow these directions, you should end up with a clone that would fool even Cosmo himself.

4 quarts water (16 cups)
6 cups chicken broth
2 potatoes, peeled and sliced
2 carrots, peeled and sliced
2 stalks celery
2 cups peeled and diced eggplant
  (about ¹/₂ of an eggplant)
1 medium onion, chopped
1 cup frozen yellow corn kernels
²/₃ cup diced canned roasted red
  pepper
¹/₂ cup tomato sauce
¹/₂ cup shelled pistachios

¹/₂ cup roasted cashews
¹/₂ cup chopped fresh Italian
  parsley
¹/₄ cup lemon juice
¹/₄ cup (¹/₂ stick) butter
3 tablespoons granulated sugar
1 teaspoon curry powder
¹/₂ teaspoon ground black pepper
¹/₄ teaspoon dried thyme
1 bay leaf
pinch dried marjoram
pinch ground nutmeg

1. Combine all the ingredients in a large pot and place over high heat.
2. Bring to a boil, then reduce the heat and simmer for 3 to 4 hours, or until the soup has reduced and is thick and brownish in color. It should have the consistency of chili. Stir occasionally for the first few hours, but stir often in the last hour. The edges of the potatoes should become rounded as they fall apart, and the nuts will soften. Serve hot.

• MAKES 4 TO 6 SERVINGS.

Tidbits

Because of the extreme reduction, I found that the salt in the chicken broth was enough for the recipe. However, if you use a low-sodium broth, you may need to add a little salt to the soup.

•   •   •   •

THE SOUP NAZI'S MEXICAN CHICKEN CHILI

☆ ✌ 💣 ✏ ☯ ✂ ☞

In *Zagat's* 1995 New York City Restaurant Survey, Le Cirque 2000, one of the city's most upscale restaurants, received a 25 rating out of a possible 30. In the same guide, Al "the Soup Nazi" Yeganeh's Soup Kitchen International scored a whopping 27. That put the Soup Nazi's eatery in 14th place among the city's best restaurants for that year!

It was common to see lines stretching around the corner and down the block as hungry patrons waited for their cup of one of five daily hot soup selections. Most of the selections changed every day, but of the three days that I was there, the Mexican Chicken Chili was always on the menu. The first two days it was sold out before I got to the front of the line. But on the last day I got lucky: "One extra-large Mexican Chicken Chili, please." Hand over money, move to the extreme left.

So here now is a clone for what has apparently become one of the Soup Nazi's most popular culinary masterpieces. The secret to this soup, as with many of his creations, seems to be the long simmering time. If you like, you can substitute turkey breast for the chicken to make turkey chili, which was the soup George Costanza ordered on *Seinfeld*.

1 pound chicken breast fillets
   (3 to 4 fillets)
1 tablespoon olive oil
10 cups water
2 cups chicken broth
1/2 cup tomato sauce

1 potato, peeled and chopped
1 small onion, diced
1 cup frozen yellow corn kernels
1/2 carrot, sliced
1 celery stalk, diced
1 cup canned diced tomatoes

one 15-ounce can red kidney
  beans, plus liquid
1/4 cup diced canned pimento
1 jalapeño pepper, diced
1/4 cup chopped fresh Italian
  parsley
1 clove garlic, minced

1 1/2 teaspoons chili powder
1 teaspoon ground cumin
1/2 teaspoon salt
pinch cayenne pepper
pinch dried basil
pinch dried oregano

ON THE SIDE

sour cream

chopped fresh Italian parsley

1. Sauté the chicken breasts in the olive oil in a large pot over medium-high heat on both sides until done, 5 to 6 minutes per side. Cool the chicken until it can be handled. Do not rinse the pot.
2. Shred the chicken by hand into bite-size pieces and place the pieces back into the pot.
3. Add the remaining ingredients to the pot and turn the heat to high. Bring the mixture to a boil, then reduce the heat and simmer for 3 to 4 hours. Stir the mixture often so that many of the chicken pieces shred into much smaller bits. The chili should reduce substantially to thicken and darken (less orange, more brown) when done.
4. Combine some chopped Italian parsley with sour cream and serve it on the side for topping the chili, if desired.

• MAKES 4 TO 6 SERVINGS.

• • • •

SPATINI
SPAGHETTI SAUCE MIX

☆　　✌　　💣　　✏　　☯　　✂　　☞

Since the Spatini Italian Foods Company discontinued production and sale of its spaghetti sauce mix in December 2006, Internet discussion groups have organized petitions pleading to bring the product back. For more than forty years generations of families have enjoyed spaghetti made by mixing a packet of top-secret powder with canned tomato sauce. But after Spatini disappeared from grocery store shelves, the only way to get that same flavor on spaghetti required locating leftover stock on the Internet—and paying dearly for it. On eBay, ten-box lots of Spatini sold for up to ten times what they originally cost in stores. Now you can save your hard-earned lira and still get real Spatini flavor, because after analyzing a packet of the mix I've discovered a great way to clone this Dead Food at even less cost than the product's retail price before it became extinct. The secret ingredient is a crushed-up beef bouillon cube, which contains the precise quantity of salt and natural flavors, plus autolyzed yeast extract (a flavor enhancer), to mirror the original blend. Add a couple ground herbs, onion, garlic, powdered sugar, and cornstarch to substitute for the potato starch used in the real thing, and you'll have the exact amount of mix you need to re-create the spaghetti sauce you grew up with.

I beef bouillon cube, crushed
1 ½ teaspoons powdered sugar
1 teaspoon cornstarch
¼ teaspoon ground oregano

¼ teaspoon ground thyme
¼ teaspoon onion powder
⅛ teaspoon garlic powder
pinch ground black pepper

Pulverize the beef bouillon cube to a powder using a kitchen mallet or mortar and pestle. Mix with remaining ingredients in a small bowl. To make spaghetti sauce, follow the same instructions that appear on the original box of Spatini:

1. In a medium saucepan, combine the seasoning mix, 1 tablespoon oil (optional), desired tomatoes, and amount of water listed on chart.
2. Bring to a boil, then simmer, stirring frequently, as directed below.
3. Makes about 1 pint of sauce—4 (½ cup) servings.

Tomatoes	Water	Simmer
1 can (6 oz.) tomato paste	1½ cups	5 min.
1 can (15 oz.) tomato puree	¾ cup	5 min.
2 cups (16 oz.) crushed tomatoes	½ cup	15 min.
2 cups (16 oz.) carton pack tomatoes	omit	15 min.

For a Spicier Tomato Sauce

Tomatoes	Water	Simmer
1 can (15 oz.) tomato sauce	½ cup	15 min.

For a Chunky Homestyle Spaghetti Sauce

Tomatoes	Water	Simmer
1 can (14.5 oz.) whole tomatoes, cut up and undrained	½ cup	15 min.
1¼ pounds fresh ripe tomatoes, pureed	omit	40 min.

STARBUCKS
CARAMEL MACCHIATO

☆　　✌　　💧　　✏　　☯　　✂　　☞

If you've got an espresso/cappuccino machine, you're well on your way to re-creating a top-choice Starbucks coffee drink. For the caramel part, you can use any caramel sauce that you find in the grocery store near the ice-cream toppings. Pick your favorite. Just note that to make this recipe work best you'll need only 3 tablespoons of a richer caramel sauce (like the stuff Starbucks uses), but more like 4 tablespoons of a lighter sauce (such as fat-free Smuckers). For the vanilla syrup you can use the bottled syrups, such as those made by Torani, or just whip up your own clone from scratch using the recipe here. By the way, if you want to make this clone super-accurate, pick up bottles of the vanilla syrup and caramel sauce the pros use that can be found for sale in many Starbucks stores.

VANILLA SYRUP

2 cups water
1 ½ cups granulated sugar

¾ teaspoon vanilla extract

8 ounces milk, steamed with foam

½ cup fresh espresso
3 to 4 tablespoons caramel sauce

1. Combine 2 cups water and 1 ½ cups sugar in a medium saucepan and bring to a boil. Reduce the heat and simmer for 5 minutes, then add ¾ teaspoon vanilla extract. Remove from the heat and cool. Store in a covered container.

2. To make your coffee drink, add 2 tablespoons of vanilla syrup to a 16-ounce glass. Add 8 ounces of steamed milk with the foam, and then pour in the espresso.
3. Add 3 to 4 tablespoons caramel sauce to the drink. Stir before drinking.

• MAKES ONE 16-OUNCE DRINK (GRANDE SIZE).

• • • •

STARBUCKS FRAPPUCCINO (BOTTLED VERSION)

This clones Starbucks' "Low-fat Creamy Blend of Coffee and Milk" that you find in the 9½-ounce bottles in many grocery stores. Those little suckers will set you back at least a buck, but this *Top Secret Recipes* version costs a mere fraction of that. The recipe requires espresso, but don't worry if you don't have an espresso machine. Check out the Tidbits below for a way to clone espresso with a standard drip machine and ground coffee.

½ cup fresh espresso, chilled
2½ cups low-fat milk (2 percent)
¼ cup granulated sugar

1 tablespoon dry pectin (see Tidbits)

Combine all the ingredients in a pitcher or covered container. Stir or shake until the sugar is dissolved. Chill and serve cold.

- MAKES 24 OUNCES (2½ SERVINGS).

Tidbits

To fake espresso with a drip coffeemaker and standard grind of coffee: Use ⅓ cup ground coffee and 1 cup of water. Brew once, then run coffee through the machine again, keeping the same grounds. Makes about ½ cup fresh espresso to use in the above recipe. Run a pot of water through the machine, without grounds, to clean.

Pectin is a natural thickener found in fruits that is used for canning. You can find it in the supermarket near the canning supplies. It is used in this recipe to make the drink thicker and creamier, and can be found in the original recipe. It does not add to the flavor and can be excluded if you don't care so much about duplicating the texture of the original.

To make the "Mocha" variety: Add a pinch ($\frac{1}{16}$ teaspoon) of cocoa powder to the mixture before combining.

• • • •

STARBUCKS
GINGERBREAD LATTE

☆　　✌　　💣　　✏　　☯　　✂　　☞

As the holidays come around, so too does this incredible latte from Starbucks. Into the coffeehouse's basic latte recipe go a few pumps of special gingerbread-flavored syrup, and we soon experience the combined sensation of munching on a gingerbread cookie while sipping hot, milky java. To re-create the experience at home for the holidays for much less than the cost of the real thing, all we have to do is make our own gingerbread syrup with a few common ingredients. When the syrup is done, simply brew some espresso in your espresso machine, steam some hot milk, and throw it all in a cup. Top off your latte with whipped cream and a pinch of nutmeg as they do at the store, and you'll fool anyone with this hot little clone. By the way, this recipe is for a single grande-size latte, but you'll have enough syrup for as many as seven drinks.

GINGERBREAD SYRUP

2 cups water
1 1/2 cups granulated sugar
2 teaspoons ground ginger

1/2 teaspoon ground cinnamon
1/2 teaspoon vanilla extract

1/2 cup fresh espresso
8 ounces milk, steamed (with a little foam)

GARNISH

whipped cream

ground nutmeg

1. Make the gingerbread syrup by combining the water, sugar, ginger, cinnamon, and vanilla in a medium saucepan. Be sure the pan is not too small or the mixture could easily bubble over.
2. Bring the mixture to a boil, then reduce the heat and simmer the syrup uncovered for 15 minutes. Remove the syrup from the heat when it's done and slap a lid on it.
3. Make a double shot of espresso (½ cup) using an espresso machine. Use the machine to steam 8 ounces of milk, or heat up the milk in the microwave if your machine does not foam and steam milk.
4. Make your latte by first adding ½ cup espresso to a 16-ounce cup. Add ¼ cup gingerbread syrup, followed by the steamed milk. Stir.
5. Top off the drink with a dollop of whipped cream and a sprinkle of nutmeg.

- MAKES 1 GRANDE LATTE (16 OUNCES).

•   •   •   •

STARBUCKS
HOT CHOCOLATE

☆　　✌　　💣　　✎　　☯　　✂　　☞

Starbucks makes its hot chocolate with mocha syrup that's used for a variety of other drinks in the store. A barista combines mocha syrup with a couple squirts of vanilla syrup and heated milk, and he then finishes off the drink with a sweet pile of whipped cream. We can duplicate the process by first creating our own chocolate syrup in the microwave with cocoa—Hershey or Nestlé brand each works great. After adding milk to our heated chocolate mixture, we pop it back into the microwave again until piping hot. A little vanilla extract added at the end gives the drink the vanilla hints of the original. I found that a 2-cup glass measuring cup with a spout works best to heat the drink in the microwave. Then, when it's ready, you can easily pour the hot chocolate into a 16-ounce coffee mug and get on with the sipping.

¹/₄ cup water
2 tablespoons unsweetened
   cocoa powder

2 tablespoons granulated sugar
1 ¹/₂ cups milk
¹/₄ teaspoon vanilla extract

GARNISH
whipped cream

1. Combine the water, cocoa, and sugar in a 16-ounce microwave-safe pitcher, such as a 2-cup glass measuring cup. Zap the mixture on high for 30 seconds, or until hot. Stir well to create chocolate syrup.
2. Add the milk to the chocolate syrup and microwave the mix-

ture for 1 to 1½ minutes, or until hot. Add the vanilla and pour the drink into a 16-ounce coffee mug. Serve with whipped cream on top.

- MAKES 1 GRANDE-SIZE SERVING (16 OUNCES).

•   •   •   •

STARBUCKS MOCHA COCONUT FRAPPUCCINO

This discontinued Starbucks delight is like a cold Mounds bar in a cup—it's surprising that the ultra-delicious iced coffee drink was nixed from the menu. Good thing we have a clone. Find shredded coconut in the baking aisle and toast ½ cup of it (store the leftover coconut in the fridge). You'll use most of the toasted coconut in the blender, but save a little for the garnish when the drinks are done.

½ cup sweetened shredded
   coconut
¾ cup double-strength coffee
1 cup low-fat milk

⅓ cup Hershey's chocolate syrup
3 tablespoons granulated sugar
2 cups ice

GARNISH
whipped cream

1. Preheat the oven to 300 degrees F. Spread the shredded coconut on a baking sheet and toast the coconut in the oven. Stir the coconut around every 10 minutes or so for even browning. After 25 to 30 minutes, the shredded coconut should be light brown. Cool it off.
2. Make double-strength coffee by brewing with twice the coffee required by your coffeemaker. That should be 2 tablespoons of ground coffee per each cup of coffee. Chill before using.
3. To make the drinks, combine the cold coffee, milk, ⅓ cup of the toasted coconut, the chocolate syrup, and sugar in a blender. Blend for 15 to 20 seconds to dissolve the sugar. Add the ice and

blend until the ice is crushed and the drink is smooth. Pour into two 16-ounce glasses. Garnish each drink with whipped cream, a drizzle of chocolate, and a pinch of some of the remaining toasted coconut. Add a straw to each one.

- MAKES 2 GRANDE-SIZE DRINKS (16 OUNCES EACH).

•　•　•　•

STARBUCKS CARROT CAKE

☆　✌　💣　✎　☯　✂　☞

There's nothing like a slice of fresh carrot cake with cream cheese frosting and a tall glass of cold milk. A hot latte ain't such a bad chaser either. I suppose that's why you'll find one of the best carrot cakes at Starbucks. It's moist and flavorful, packed with nuts and golden raisins. Starbucks makes sure its tasty baked goods are fresh by contracting with local bakeries to produce cakes and scones and muffins from the coffee chain's top-secret specs. Now you've got your own secret specs with this formula for a carrot cake clone that tastes like it came straight from your local coffeehouse.

CAKE

1 1/2 cups all-purpose flour
2 teaspoons baking powder
1 teaspoon baking soda
2 teaspoons ground cinnamon
1/2 teaspoon salt
1/4 teaspoon ground nutmeg
1/4 teaspoon ground allspice
1 1/2 cups dark brown sugar

1 cup vegetable oil
3 eggs
1/4 teaspoon vanilla extract
1 cup shredded carrot (1 large carrot)
3/4 cup chopped walnuts
1/2 cup golden raisins

FROSTING

8 ounces cream cheese, softened
1 tablespoon milk

1 teaspoon vanilla extract
3 cups powdered sugar

DRIZZLE

2 ounces white chocolate, melted

(1/3 cup)

GARNISH
⅓ cup chopped pecans

1. Preheat the oven to 350 degrees F.
2. To make the cake, sift together the flour, baking powder, baking soda, cinnamon, salt, nutmeg, and allspice in a large bowl.
3. Use an electric mixer to combine the brown sugar and oil. Add the eggs and vanilla and beat on high speed for about 1 minute.
4. Combine the wet mixture with the dry stuff. Mix on low speed until all the ingredients are incorporated, then crank up the speed and blend on high until batter is smooth.
5. Add the shredded carrot, walnuts, and raisins and mix by hand. Pour the batter into a 9 × 13-inch baking pan that has been generously greased with shortening.
6. Bake for 40 to 50 minutes, or until a toothpick stuck in the center comes out clean. Allow the cake to cool completely.
7. Make the frosting by mixing the softened cream cheese, milk, and vanilla in a large bowl with an electric mixer. Add the powdered sugar, 1 cup at a time, and blend well until the frosting is smooth.
8. When the cake has cooled, frost the top with the entire bowl of cream cheese frosting. Melt the white chocolate and drizzle it over the cake using a squirt bottle or a small storage bag with the tip of a corner cut off. Sprinkle the pecans over the frosting. Slice into 12 pieces to serve. Cover the leftover cake and store it in the fridge.

- MAKES 12 SERVINGS.

•   •   •   •

STARBUCKS CLASSIC COFFEE CAKE

☆ ✌ 💣 ✏ ☯ ✂ ☞

A good coffeehouse will have good coffee cake, and Starbucks is no exception. The world's biggest coffee chain offers cake that is moist and buttery, with a perfect cinnamon streusel crumb topping and a strip of cinnamon sugar through the middle. You may find slight variations of the cake at different Starbucks locations. Sometimes the cake is topped with chopped pecans, and some may be dusted on top with a little powdered sugar. The recipe below clones the basic recipe, and if you want nuts on top, mix ½ cup of chopped pecans into the streusel topping before adding it.

TOPPING
1 cup all-purpose flour
1 cup packed light brown sugar

1 ¼ teaspoons ground cinnamon
½ cup (1 stick) butter, softened

OPTIONAL (FOR TOPPING)
½ cup chopped pecans

CINNAMON SUGAR
⅓ cup light brown sugar
¾ teaspoon ground cinnamon
¾ cup butter, softened
⅓ cup packed light brown sugar
½ cup granulated sugar
2 eggs
1 tablespoon vegetable oil

1 ½ teaspoons vanilla extract
2 cups all-purpose flour
1 teaspoon baking powder
¼ teaspoon baking soda
¼ teaspoon salt
⅓ cup buttermilk
⅓ cup whole milk

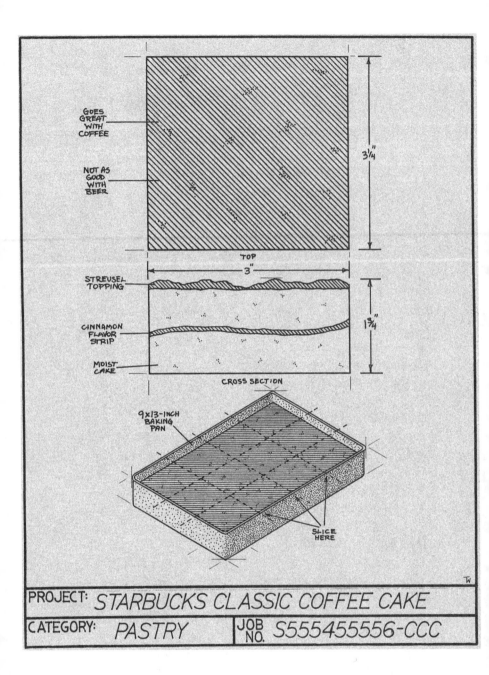

GOES GREAT WITH COFFEE

NOT AS GOOD WITH BEER

TOP

3¼"

STREUSEL TOPPING

CINNAMON FLAVOR STRIP

MOIST CAKE

3"

1¾"

CROSS SECTION

9x13-INCH BAKING PAN

SLICE HERE

TW

PROJECT: *STARBUCKS CLASSIC COFFEE CAKE*

CATEGORY: *PASTRY*   **JOB NO.** *S555455556-CCC*

1. Preheat the oven to 325 degrees F.
2. Make topping by combining the flour with the brown sugar and cinnamon in a medium bowl. Mix in the softened butter and use your hands to combine until the mixture is crumbly and has the consistency of moist sand.
3. Make the cinnamon sugar that will go in the middle of the cake by combining the light brown sugar with the cinnamon in a small bowl.
4. In a large bowl, cream together the butter, $\frac{1}{3}$ cup packed light brown sugar, and the granulated sugar with an electric mixer for 1 minute. Add the eggs, oil, and vanilla and mix until fluffy.
5. In a separate bowl, combine the flour, baking powder, baking soda, and salt. Combine this dry mixture with the bowl of moist ingredients. Add the buttermilk and milk and mix well.
6. Spoon half the batter into a 9 x 13-inch baking pan that has been buttered and dusted with a light coating of flour. Sprinkle the cinnamon sugar over the batter and pat it down into the batter. Spread the rest of the batter over the crumb topping. You may have to moisten your hands with warm water or coat them with a little oil to move the batter around so that it spreads out to the edges of the pan.
7. Sprinkle the topping over the batter, making sure that the topping evenly covers all the batter.
8. Bake the cake for 50 to 55 minutes, or until the edges just begin to turn light brown. Cool and slice into 12 pieces.

- SERVES 12.

•   •   •   •

STARBUCKS CRANBERRY BLISS BAR

☆ ✌ 💣 ✏ ☻ ✂ ☞

Each holiday season Starbucks brings out one of its most beloved dessert recipes: a soft triangle of white chocolate and cranberry cake covered with delicious creamy lemon frosting and dried cranberries. But when the holidays are over, the Bliss Bars go back into hiding until next season. That's when we bust out our home clone. The cake is flavored with bits of crystallized ginger that you can find in most markets near the herbs and spices. Be sure to finely mince the chunks of ginger before adding them, since ginger has a strong flavor and you don't want anyone biting into a whole chunk. For the white chocolate, one 4-ounce bar of Ghirardelli white chocolate will give you the perfect amount of chunks after you chop it up. If you can't find that brand, any brand of white chocolate will do, or you can use 4 ounces of white chocolate chips. This clone recipe will make a total of 16 cake bars, at a fraction of the cost of the original.

CAKE

¾ cup (1½ sticks) butter, softened
1¼ cups packed light brown
  sugar
3 eggs
2 tablespoons minced crystallized
  ginger
1½ teaspoons vanilla extract

½ teaspoon salt
1½ cups all-purpose flour
½ teaspoon baking powder
¾ cup chopped sweetened dried
  cranberries
4 ounces white chocolate, cut into
  chunks

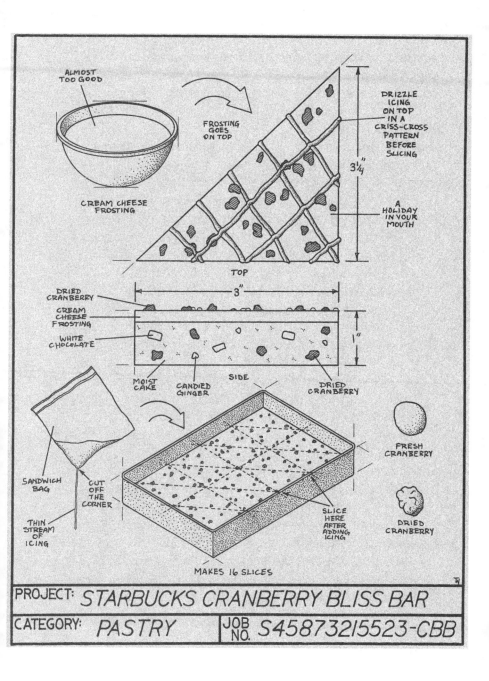

ALMOST
TOO GOOD

FROSTING
GOES
ON TOP

DRIZZLE
ICING
ON TOP
IN A
CRISS-CROSS
PATTERN
BEFORE
SLICING

3¼"

A
HOLIDAY
IN YOUR
MOUTH

CREAM CHEESE
FROSTING

TOP

DRIED
CRANBERRY

CREAM
CHEESE
FROSTING

WHITE
CHOCOLATE

3"

1"

MOIST
CAKE

CANDIED
GINGER

SIDE

DRIED
CRANBERRY

SANDWICH
BAG

CUT
OFF
THE
CORNER

THIN
STREAM
OF
ICING

FRESH
CRANBERRY

SLICE
HERE
AFTER
ADDING
ICING

DRIED
CRANBERRY

MAKES 16 SLICES

PROJECT: *STARBUCKS CRANBERRY BLISS BAR*

CATEGORY: *PASTRY*   JOB NO. *S45873215523-CBB*

FROSTING

4 ounces cream cheese, softened
3 cups powdered sugar
4 teaspoons lemon juice

1 teaspoon vanilla extract
$1/4$ cup chopped sweetened dried
   cranberries

DRIZZLED ICING

$1/2$ cup powdered sugar
1 tablespoon milk

2 teaspoons vegetable shortening

1. Preheat the oven to 350 degrees F.
2. Make cake by beating the butter and brown sugar together with an electric mixer until smooth. Add the eggs, ginger, vanilla, and salt and beat well. Gradually mix in the flour and baking powder until smooth. Mix the chopped dried cranberries and white chocolate chunks into the batter by hand. Pour the batter into a buttered 9 x 13-inch baking pan. Use a spatula to spread the batter evenly across the pan. Bake for 25 to 30 minutes, or until the cake is lightly browned on top. Allow the cake to cool.
3. Make the frosting by combining the softened cream cheese, powdered sugar, lemon juice, and vanilla in a medium bowl with an electric mixer until smooth. When the cake has cooled, use a spatula to spread the frosting over the top of the cake.
4. Sprinkle ¼ cup of chopped dried cranberries over the frosting on the cake.
5. Make the drizzled icing by whisking together the powdered sugar, milk, and shortening. Drizzle this icing over the cranberries in a sweeping motion with a squirt bottle or fill a small plastic storage bag with the icing and cut off the tip of one corner.
6. Cover the cake and let it chill out in the fridge for a couple of hours, then slice the cake lengthwise (the long way) through the middle. Slice the cake across the width three times, making a total of eight rectangular slices. Slice each of those rectangles diagonally creating 16 triangular slices.

- MAKES 16 BARS.

•   •   •   •

STARBUCKS LEMON LOAF

It would take quite a bit of real lemon juice to give this moist cake loaf clone the perfect lemony zip of the original. With too much liquid we wind up with thin batter and ultimately a baked lemon loaf that lacks the dense and flavorful quality of the coffeehouse original. So, to avoid producing a batter that's too runny, we must turn to lemon extract. It's over by the vanilla extract in the baking aisle. This concentrated lemon flavoring works well alongside real lemon juice to give us the perfectly intense lemon flavor we need for a killer clone. The lemon extract also works like a charm to flavor the icing that will top off your faux food.

LEMON LOAF

1 ½ cups all-purpose flour
½ teaspoon baking soda
½ teaspoon baking powder
½ teaspoon salt
3 eggs
1 cup granulated sugar

2 tablespoons butter, softened
1 teaspoon vanilla extract
1 teaspoon lemon extract
⅓ cup lemon juice
½ cup vegetable oil

LEMON ICING

1 cup plus 1 tablespoon
  powdered sugar

2 tablespoons whole milk
½ teaspoon lemon extract

1. Preheat the oven to 350 degrees F.
2. To make the loaf, combine the flour, baking soda, baking powder, and salt in a large bowl.

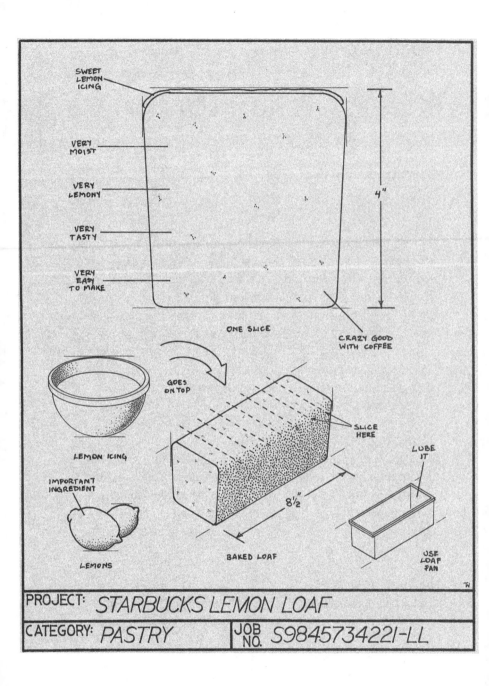

SWEET LEMON ICING

VERY MOIST

VERY LEMONY

VERY TASTY

VERY EASY TO MAKE

4"

ONE SLICE

CRAZY GOOD WITH COFFEE

GOES ON TOP

LEMON ICING

IMPORTANT INGREDIENT

LEMONS

SLICE HERE

8½"

BAKED LOAF

LUBE IT

USE LOAF PAN

PROJECT: *STARBUCKS LEMON LOAF*

CATEGORY: *PASTRY*   **JOB NO.** *S9845734221-LL*

3. Use an electric mixer to blend together eggs, sugar, butter, vanilla, lemon extract, and lemon juice in a medium bowl.

4. Pour the wet ingredients into the dry ingredients and blend until smooth. Add the oil and mix well.

5. Pour the ingredients into a well-greased 8½ x 4½ -inch loaf pan. Bake for 45 minutes, or until a toothpick stuck into the center of the cake comes out clean.

6. Make the lemon icing by combining the ingredients in a small bowl with electric mixer on low speed. When the lemon loaf has cooled, remove it from the pan and frost the top with the lemon icing. When the icing has set up, slice the loaf into eight 1-inch-thick slices.

- MAKES 8 SLICES.

•   •   •   •

STARBUCKS
MAPLE OAT NUT SCONE

☆   ✌   💣   ✎   ◉   ✂   ☞

As far as scones go, the maple oat nut scone at Starbucks is a superstar. It's flaky, yet it has a bit of a chewy texture from the oats and the nuts, plus a not-too-strong maple flavor both in the scone and in the icing on top. At first I thought that we could use real maple syrup for a good clone or even the maple-flavored syrups that are more commonly used on pancakes today (they are actually corn syrup based and artificially flavored). But I found that these syrups add too much moisture to the dough, creating something more like cake batter than the type of dough we want for a dense, chewy scone. In this case I found that the caramel-colored imitation maple flavoring stocked near the vanilla extract in your supermarket gives this scone—and the icing—the strong maple taste and dark caramel color that perfectly matches the flavor and appearance of the real deal.

SCONE

2 1/2 cups all-purpose flour
1/2 cup rolled oats (not instant)
1 tablespoon baking powder
1 teaspoon ground cinnamon
1/2 teaspoon salt
4 tablespoons cold butter

1/3 cup chopped walnuts
1 large egg
2/3 cup dark brown sugar
1/4 cup half-and-half
2 teaspoons imitation maple
  flavoring

MAPLE ICING

1 cup powdered sugar
4 teaspoons whole milk

1/2 teaspoon imitation maple
  flavoring

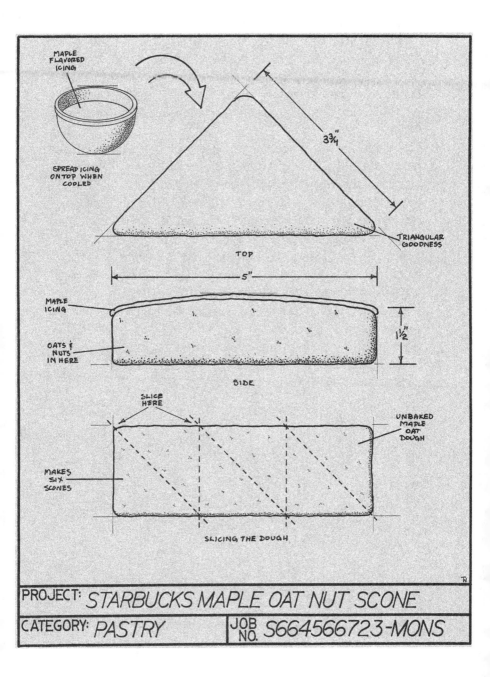

MAPLE
FLAVORED
ICING

SPREAD ICING
ON TOP WHEN
COOLED

3¾"

TRIANGULAR
GOODNESS

TOP

5"

MAPLE
ICING

OATS &
NUTS
IN HERE

1½"

SIDE

SLICE
HERE

UNBAKED
MAPLE
OAT
DOUGH

MAKES
SIX
SCONES

SLICING THE DOUGH

PROJECT: STARBUCKS MAPLE OAT NUT SCONE

CATEGORY: PASTRY

JOB NO. S664566723-MONS

1. Preheat the oven to 375 degrees F.
2. To make the scones, combine the flour, oats, baking powder, cinnamon, and salt in a large bowl. Use a pastry knife or a fork to cut the cold butter into the dry mixture. Break the butter down until there are no pieces larger than a pea. Stir in the chopped walnuts.
3. Use an electric mixer to combine the egg, brown sugar, half-and-half, and maple flavoring in a medium bowl.
4. Combine the wet ingredients with dry ingredients and blend with electric mixer until firm, then use your hands to mix the dough until you can form it into a ball. Pat the dough out on a lightly floured surface until it is about 1¼ inches thick. Shape the dough into a rectangle, and then use a pizza wheel or large knife to cut the dough into 6 triangles. Arrange the dough triangles on a baking sheet and bake for 25 to 30 minutes, or just until the scones begin to turn light brown on the edges.
5. As the scones cool, combine the icing ingredients in a medium bowl with an electric mixer on low speed. When the scones have cooled, spread the icing on top of each one with a frosting knife or spatula.

• MAKES 6 SCONES.

STARBUCKS PEPPERMINT BROWNIE

☆   ✌   💣   ✏   ☯   ✂   ☞

Here's a great one for the holidays (or anytime you want, really). It's a mint chocolate brownie with peppermint buttercream frosting on top and creamy chocolate frosting on top of that. And to simplify the cloning process a bit, we start with a common fudge brownie mix. By changing the required ingredients listed on the brownie mix box and adding some other modified steps, we can improve on the finished product. Rather than oil, use a stick of melted butter in your brownies for a richer, better flavor. And cook the brownies at a slightly lower temperature so that they come out moist and chewy. Since this recipe is for peppermint brownies, adding just a bit of peppermint extract will do the trick. The peppermint brownies from Starbucks have red and white frosting drizzled lightly across the top. To save time, buy premade red and white colored frostings that come in little cans (with tips included).

BROWNIES

one 19.5-ounce box fudge
  brownie mix (Betty Crocker
  Fudge Brownie Mix works
  great)

$\frac{1}{2}$ cup (1 stick) butter, melted
$\frac{1}{4}$ cup water
2 large eggs
$\frac{1}{4}$ teaspoon peppermint extract

PEPPERMINT BUTTERCREAM FROSTING

$\frac{1}{2}$ cup (1 stick) butter, softened
1 $\frac{1}{2}$ cups powdered sugar
1 tablespoon milk

$\frac{1}{4}$ teaspoon peppermint extract
$\frac{1}{4}$ teaspoon vanilla extract

CHOCOLATE FROSTING

⅓ cup whole milk
¼ cup (½ stick) butter
one 12-ounce bag semisweet
   chocolate chips

1 teaspoon vanilla extract
1 cup powdered sugar

DECORATIVE ICING

1 can white frosting (with
   fine tip)

1 can red frosting (with fine tip)

1. Preheat the oven to 325 degrees F, then prepare a 9 x 9-inch baking pan by spraying it with a light coating of nonstick spray. Cut a piece of parchment paper or nonstick aluminum foil to the same width as the bottom of the pan, but make it much longer than the pan so that the left and right ends go up and out of the pan on the left and right sides. This will create a "sling" that will help you lift the brownies out of the pan after they've baked.
2. Make the brownie batter by first sifting the box of ingredients. This will destroy any clumps. Add the melted butter, water, eggs, and peppermint extract and mix the batter by hand just until all the dry stuff is mixed in. Pour the batter into your prepared baking pan and bake it for 50 to 55 minutes, or until a toothpick stuck in the center comes out clean. Allow the brownies to cool before frosting.
3. Make the peppermint buttercream frosting by beating together 1 cup of powdered sugar and the softened butter in a medium bowl with an electric mixer. Mix in another ½ cup of powdered sugar, then add the milk and the peppermint and vanilla extracts. Mix for about 1 minute to make the frosting smooth. Add an additional ¼ cup of powdered sugar if the frosting is too thin and light. You want a frosting that can be spread easily, yet it should be firm enough to hold up the layer of chocolate frosting that's coming next. When the brownie has cooled, use a spatula to spread the frosting evenly over the top. Put the brownie in the fridge to firm up the buttercream frosting.
4. Make the chocolate frosting by bringing the whole milk and butter to a boil in a small saucepan over medium heat. Pour the

chocolate chips into a heat-safe bowl. When the milk and butter comes to a boil, pour the mixture over the chocolate chips and let it all just sit there in the bowl for a couple minutes. Add the vanilla to the mixture and whisk until smooth. Use an electric mixer to beat in the powdered sugar until the frosting is smooth. Spread the chocolate frosting over the white frosting on the brownie.

5. Add the decorative red and white icing by first applying the white icing to the top of the cake in a sweeping motion diagonally across the top of the entire cake, then add the red icing over the white in the same sweeping motion in the same direction.

6. Stick the brownie back in the fridge for about an hour before removing it from the pan and slicing it into 9 equal portions. The leftovers will keep well for several days covered in the refrigerator.

- MAKES 9 BROWNIES.

• • • •

STARBUCKS
PUMPKIN BREAD

☆ ✌ 💣 ✏ ☯ ✂ ☞

A thick slice of moist pumpkin bread Starbucks-style is the perfect companion for your morning cup of joe. Many other pumpkin bread recipes produce sad, squatty loaves—but not this clone. Here's a custom formula that makes enough batter to fill up a medium loaf pan. And when the bread is done, you'll slice the beefy loaf into 8 thick square hunks of goodness that perfectly mimic the look and flavor of the real thing right down to the chopped pumpkin seeds on top.

1 ½ cups all-purpose flour
1 teaspoon baking soda
½ teaspoon baking powder
¾ teaspoon ground cinnamon
½ teaspoon ground ginger
¼ teaspoon ground cloves
¼ teaspoon ground allspice
½ teaspoon salt

4 eggs
1 cup granulated sugar
¼ cup dark brown sugar
½ teaspoon vanilla extract
¾ cups canned pure pumpkin
   puree
¾ cup vegetable oil
¼ cup pumpkin seeds, chopped

1. Preheat the oven to 350 degrees F.
2. Combine the flour, baking soda, baking powder, spices, and salt in a medium bowl.
3. Beat the eggs, sugars, and vanilla together in a large bowl with an electric mixer on high speed for about 30 seconds. Add the pumpkin and oil and mix well.
4. Pour the dry ingredients into the wet stuff and mix well with your electric mixer. Pour the batter into a well-greased 8½ x 4½ -inch loaf pan. Sprinkle the chopped pumpkin seeds over the

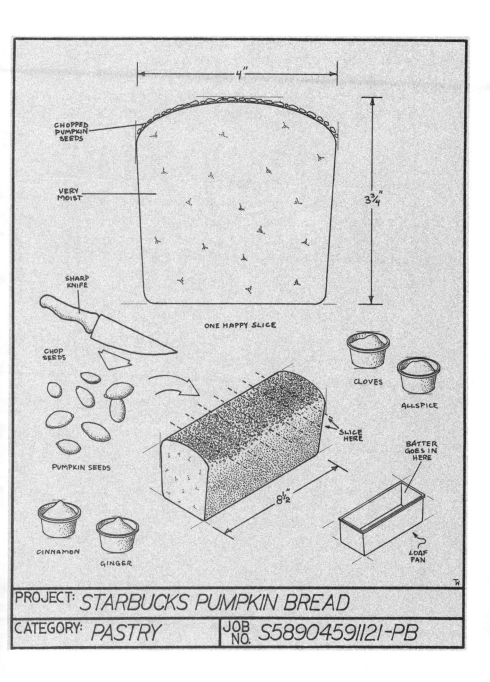

4"

CHOPPED
PUMPKIN
SEEDS

VERY
MOIST

3¾"

ONE HAPPY SLICE

SHARP
KNIFE

CHOP
SEEDS

PUMPKIN SEEDS

CLOVES

ALLSPICE

SLICE
HERE

BATTER
GOES IN
HERE

8½"

CINNAMON

GINGER

LOAF
PAN

PROJECT: *STARBUCKS PUMPKIN BREAD*

CATEGORY: *PASTRY*   JOB NO. *S58904591121-PB*

top of the batter, and then bake for 60 minutes or until the top of the bread is beginning to brown and a toothpick stuck into the center of the bread comes out clean.

5. When the bread has cooled, remove it from the loaf pan and use a bread knife to slice it into approximately 1-inch-thick slices.

• MAKES 8 SLICES.

Tidbits

This bread freezes perfectly. Simply seal any leftover slices in a zip-top bag or wrap them in plastic and pop them into the icebox. To serve, microwave one frozen slice on high for about 45 seconds and it'll taste like it just came out of the oven.

• • • •

STARBUCKS PUMPKIN CREAM CHEESE MUFFIN

☆ ✌ 💣 ✏ 👁 ✂ ☞

This delicious fall offering arrives frozen to each Starbucks store and is thawed out just before opening in the morning. The pumpkin cream cheese muffins were especially popular in the fall of 2008. According to my local Starbucks manager, a memo fired off to all stores warned of a shortage in the product and that inventory in most states would be depleted before the holidays arrived. That was enough information to get me quickly working on a clone recipe, and here you have it! First, sweeten some cream cheese and get it back in the fridge to firm up. It's much easier to work into the top of the muffins when it's cold. The pumpkin seeds that are sprinkled on top of each muffin get candied in a large skillet with brown sugar and cinnamon. Line a 12-cup muffin tin with paper muffin cups, add the muffin batter and some cream cheese, top with the candied pumpkins seeds, and then bake. Soon you'll have a dozen fresh clones of the amazing muffins, and you'll always be prepared for the next pumpkin cream cheese muffin shortage.

SWEET CREAM CHEESE
4 ounces cream cheese, softened
2 tablespoons granulated sugar
$^1/_4$ teaspoon vanilla extract

CANDIED PUMPKIN SEEDS
2 tablespoons light brown sugar
1 tablespoon water
$^1/_4$ teaspoon ground cinnamon
3 tablespoons shelled pumpkin seeds (pepitas)

MUFFIN BATTER

1 1/2 cups all-purpose flour
1 teaspoon baking powder
1 teaspoon baking soda
1 1/2 teaspoons ground cinnamon
1 teaspoon ground ginger
1/2 teaspoon ground cloves
1/2 teaspoon ground allspice
1/2 teaspoon salt

3 eggs
3/4 cup dark brown sugar
1/2 cup granulated sugar
1 teaspoon vanilla extract
1 cup canned pure pumpkin
  puree
3/4 cup vegetable oil

YOU WILL ALSO NEED

12 paper muffin cups

1. Make the sweet cream cheese by using an electric mixer to combine 4 ounces cream cheese with the sugar and vanilla in a medium bowl. Mix until smooth, and then cover and chill until firm.
2. Preheat the oven to 350 degrees F.
3. Make the candied pumpkin seeds by combining the light brown sugar, water, and cinnamon in a medium skillet and place over medium heat. Add the pumpkin seeds and stir constantly as the water evaporates and the sugar crystallizes on the nuts, about 2 minutes. When you see the sugar starting to harden on the seeds, immediately turn off the heat and pour them out onto a plate to cool. Separate any seeds that are stuck together.
4. To make the muffin batter, combine the flour, baking powder, baking soda, cinnamon, ginger, cloves, allspice, and salt in a medium bowl.
5. In a large bowl, use an electric mixer to combine the eggs, sugars, and vanilla. Mix for about 30 seconds, and then add the pumpkin and oil. Mix again for another 30 seconds. Add the bowl of dry ingredients to the wet ingredients and mix well for 30 seconds, or until batter is smooth.
6. Spoon the batter into paper muffin cups lining a 12-cup muffin tin. The batter should be level with the top of each cup. Scoop up approximately 1 tablespoon of the sweetened cream cheese with a teaspoon and use your fingers to press it down into the

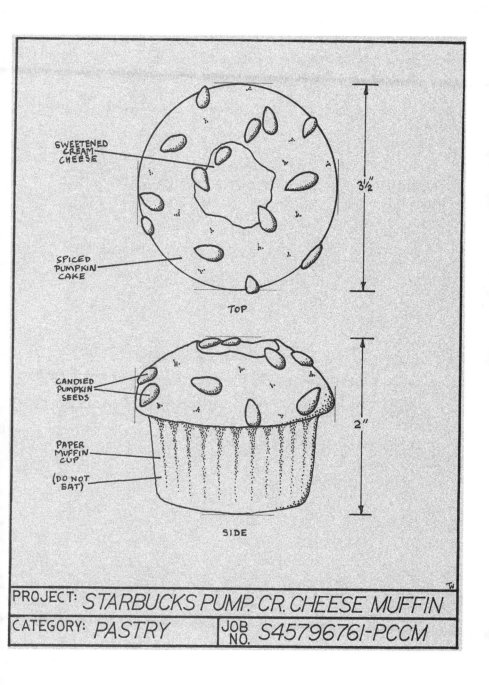

SWEETENED
CREAM-
CHEESE

SPICED
PUMPKIN
CAKE

3½"

TOP

CANDIED
PUMPKIN
SEEDS

PAPER
MUFFIN
CUP

(DO NOT
EAT)

2"

SIDE

TW

PROJECT: *STARBUCKS PUMP. CR. CHEESE MUFFIN*

CATEGORY: *PASTRY* JOB NO. *S45796761-PCCM*

middle of each cup of batter. Sprinkle some candied pumpkin seeds over each muffin and bake for 20 to 25 minutes, until lightly browned on top and a toothpick stuck into the center of a muffin comes out clean.

• MAKES 1 DOZEN MUFFINS.

Tidbits

These muffins freeze well for several months. Defrost at room temperature for 1 to 1½ hours before serving.

•   •   •   •

STARBUCKS
PUMPKIN SCONE

☆　　✌　　💣　　✏　　☯　　✂　　☞

During the holiday months you'd better get over to Starbucks bright and early if you want to get your teeth around a delicious pumpkin scone. These orange triangles of goodness are made with real pumpkin and pumpkin pie spices, and they quickly vanish out the door when fall rolls around. Each scone is generously coated with a simple plain glaze and then spiced icing is drizzled over the top for the perfect finishing touch. But good scones are more than just good flavor. To get the flaky texture cut cold butter into the dry ingredients, either with a pastry knife and some elbow grease, or by pulsing away at it with a food processor, until all the butter chunks have been worked in.

SCONE

2 cups all-purpose flour
7 tablespoons granulated sugar
1 tablespoon baking powder
$^1/_2$ teaspoon salt
$^1/_2$ teaspoon ground cinnamon
$^1/_2$ teaspoon ground nutmeg
$^1/_4$ teaspoon ground cloves

$^1/_4$ teaspoon ground ginger
$^1/_2$ cup canned pure pumpkin
  puree
3 tablespoons half-and-half
1 large egg
6 tablespoons cold butter

PLAIN GLAZE

1 cup plus 1 tablespoon
  powdered sugar

2 tablespoons whole milk

SPICED ICING

1 cup plus 3 tablespoons powdered sugar	$^1/_8$ teaspoon ground nutmeg
2 tablespoons whole milk	pinch ground ginger
$^1/_4$ teaspoon ground cinnamon	pinch ground cloves

1. Preheat the oven to 425 degrees F.
2. Combine the flour, sugar, baking powder, salt, cinnamon, nutmeg, cloves, and ginger in a large bowl.
3. In a separate medium bowl, whisk together the pumpkin, half-and-half, and egg.
4. Cut the butter into cubes, and then add it to the dry ingredients. Use a pastry knife or a fork to combine the butter with the dry ingredients. Continue mixing until no chunks of butter are visible. You can also use a food processor: Pulse the butter into dry ingredients until it is the texture of cornmeal or coarse sand.
5. Fold the wet ingredients into the dry ingredients, then form the dough into a ball. Pat out the dough onto a lightly floured surface and form it into a 1-inch-thick rectangle that is about 9 inches long and 3 inches wide. Use a large knife or a pizza wheel to slice the dough twice through the width, making three equal portions. Cut those three slices diagonally so that you have 6 triangular slices of dough.
6. Bake for 14 to 16 minutes on a baking sheet that has been lightly oiled or lined with parchment paper. The scones should begin to turn light brown.
7. While scones cool, prepare the plain glaze by combining the ingredients in a medium bowl with an electric mixer on medium speed. Mix until smooth.
8. When the scones have cooled, use a brush to paint a coating of the glaze over the top of each scone.
9. As that white glaze firms up, prepare the spiced icing by combining the ingredients in another medium bowl with an electric mixer on medium speed. Drizzle this spiced icing over each scone using a pastry bag with a fine tip. You can create a cheap and disposable pastry bag by spooning the icing into a small

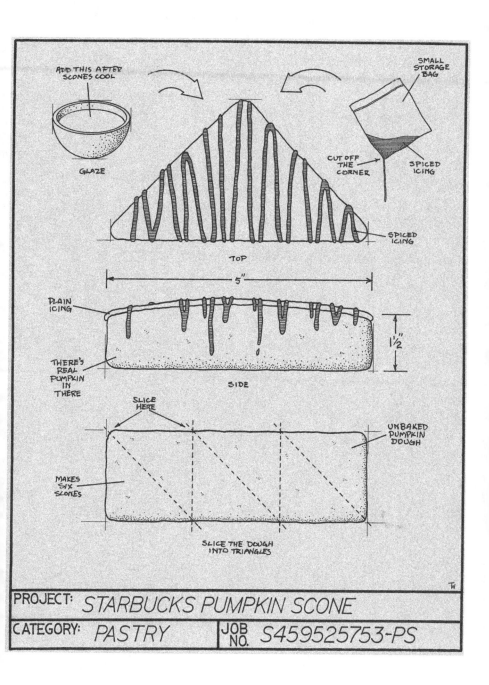

ADD THIS AFTER SCONES COOL

GLAZE

SMALL STORAGE BAG

CUT OFF THE CORNER

SPICED ICING

SPICED ICING

TOP

5"

PLAIN ICING

THERE'S REAL PUMPKIN IN THERE

SIDE

1½"

SLICE HERE

UNBAKED PUMPKIN DOUGH

MAKES SIX SCONES

SLICE THE DOUGH INTO TRIANGLES

TW

PROJECT: *STARBUCKS PUMPKIN SCONE*

CATEGORY: *PASTRY*

JOB NO. *S459525753-PS*

storage bag, then snipping the tip of a corner off the bag and gently squeezing the icing through the very small hole. Allow the icing to dry for at least 1 hour before serving.

- MAKES 6 SCONES.

•   •   •   •

STARBUCKS
VANILLA ALMOND BISCOTTI

☆　　✌　　💣　　✏　　☯　　✂　　☞

This gargantuan coffee chain has local bakers whip up many of the pastries and baked goods you see displayed behind the glass. That means everything gets to the stores real fresh, but we also find slight variations in many of the products at Starbucks in different cities. These crunchy biscotti cookies, however, are the same at every location since they have a longer shelf life and can be made in bulk at a central bakery, then individually wrapped in plastic and shipped to each store. "Biscotti" is Italian for "twice baked." The dough is first baked as one giant rectangular cookie loaf, then the loaf is removed from the oven while it's still soft, and it's sliced. These slices are arranged on a baking sheet and cooked once again until crispy. That's how the cookies get their thin profile and crunchiness, making them the perfect coffee-dunking pastry. These homemade biscotti cookies are actually best the next day after they completely dry out, as long as you live in a dry climate. If your weather is humid, be sure to seal up the cookies in a tight container after they cool so that they stay crunchy.

3 tablespoons butter
$^2/_3$ cup granulated sugar
1 egg plus 1 egg white
$^1/_2$ teaspoon vanilla extract
$^1/_4$ teaspoon salt

3 tablespoons buttermilk
1 $^3/_4$ cups all-purpose flour
2 teaspoons baking powder
1 teaspoon baking soda
$^1/_2$ cup finely chopped almonds

1. Preheat the oven to 350 degrees F.
2. Cream together the butter and sugar in a large bowl until

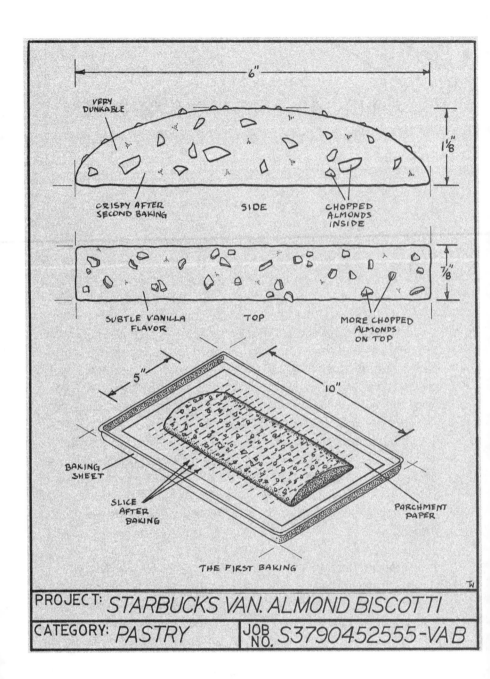

6"

VERY
DUNKABLE

1 1/8"

CRISPY AFTER
SECOND BAKING

SIDE

CHOPPED
ALMONDS
INSIDE

7/8"

SUBTLE VANILLA
FLAVOR

TOP

MORE CHOPPED
ALMONDS
ON TOP

5"

10"

BAKING
SHEET

SLICE
AFTER
BAKING

PARCHMENT
PAPER

THE FIRST BAKING

TW

PROJECT: *STARBUCKS VAN. ALMOND BISCOTTI*

CATEGORY: *PASTRY*   JOB NO. *S3790452555-VAB*

smooth. Add the egg and egg white and continue beating until creamy, then add the vanilla, salt, and buttermilk and mix until combined.

3. Sift the flour, baking powder, and baking soda together into a medium bowl. Add the dry stuff to the wet stuff in the bowl, but do it a little at a time. When all the flour's in, toss in the finely chopped almonds, but save a couple of tablespoons of the nuts for something we'll do later. Don't mix this dough too much or it might toughen up; you want to mix it only enough to get all the ingredients incorporated, and then you'll have tender biscotti. You may want to use your hands to work everything together as the dough thickens.

4. Form the dough into a rectangular loaf on a lightly greased or parchment paper–lined sheet pan. The dimensions of the loaf should be somewhere around 10 inches long and 5 inches wide, and about 1 inch thick in the middle. Sprinkle the leftover almond bits over the top of the loaf, then bake it for 30 to 35 minutes, or until the top has turned light brown. Remove this now puffed-up loaf from the oven and let it cool for 5 minutes, or as long as it takes for it to be cool enough to handle and slice.

5. When it has cooled, move the biscotti loaf to a cutting board. Use a long serrated bread knife to slice the dough across its width. Make slices that are approximately ¾ inch thick. Keep the slices standing up and move them back to the sheet pan. Position them in rows on the pan so that they aren't touching, then pop the whole pan back into the oven for 10 to 15 minutes, or until the cookies are crisp on the outside. When you remove the cookies from the oven, keep them out on the sheet pan for several hours or overnight so that they completely dry out, unless you live in a humid area. In that case, you may want to seal up the cookies immediately after they have cooled. Good biscotti are crispy biscotti.

• MAKES 20 BISCOTTI.

•   •   •   •   •

STOUFFER'S
MACARONI & CHEESE

☆   ✌   💣   ✏   ☯   ✂   ☞

What is it about Stouffer's Macaroni & Cheese that makes it the number one choice for true mac & cheese maniacs? It's probably the simple recipe that includes wholesome ingredients like skim milk and real cheddar cheese, without any preservatives or unpronounceable chemicals in there. This basic formula is good news for kitchen cloners who want an easy fix that doesn't require much shopping. I found the recipe to work best as an exact duplicate of the actual product: a frozen dish that you heat up later in the oven. This way you'll get slightly browned macaroni & cheese that looks like it posed for the nicely lit photo on the Stouffer's box. Since you'll only need about ¾ cup of uncooked elbow macaroni for each recipe, you can make several 4-person servings with just one 16-ounce box of macaroni, and then keep them all in the freezer until the days when your troops assemble for their mac attacks. Be sure to use freshly shredded cheddar cheese here, since it melts much better than pre-shredded cheese (and it's cheaper!). And use a whisk to stir the sauce often as it thickens, so that you get a smooth—not lumpy or grainy—finished product. If you feel like classing up this comfort food clone, serve it in your nicest casserole dish and tell everyone you prepared "pasta formaggio."

I cup skim milk	2 teaspoons margarine
5 teaspoons all-purpose flour	¼ teaspoon plus ⅛ teaspoon salt
2 cups (6 ounces) shredded medium cheddar cheese	¾ cups uncooked elbow macaroni (about 1¾ cups cooked)

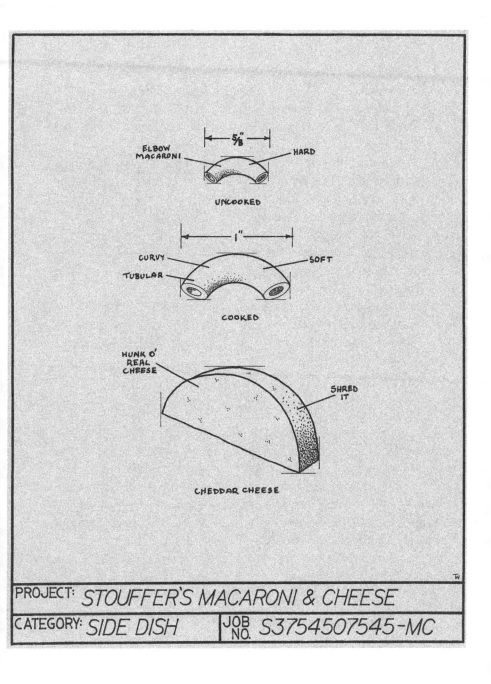

ELBOW
MACARONI

5/8"

HARD

UNCOOKED

CURVY

TUBULAR

1"

SOFT

COOKED

HUNK O'
REAL
CHEESE

SHRED
IT

CHEDDAR CHEESE

W

PROJECT: *STOUFFER'S MACARONI & CHEESE*

CATEGORY: *SIDE DISH*   JOB NO. *S3754507545-MC*

1. Whisk the flour into the skim milk in a small saucepan, then place it over medium-low heat.
2. Add the shredded cheddar cheese, margarine, and salt and stir often with a spoon until the cheese begins to melt. Reduce the heat to low and simmer for 30 minutes. Use a whisk to stir the sauce every couple of minutes so that it becomes smooth and thick.
3. While the sauce thickens, prepare the macaroni by dumping ¾ cup uncooked elbow macaroni into rapidly boiling water. Boil for 8 minutes, or until tender, and then strain. You should have about 1¾ cups of cooked macaroni.
4. When the cheese sauce has simmered for 30 minutes, pour the pasta into a medium bowl. Gently stir in the cheese sauce, and then pour mixture into a loaf pan or casserole dish. Cover and freeze.
5. When you are ready to dive into your macaroni & cheese, pre-heat the oven to 350 degrees F. Bake the frozen macaroni for 50 to 53 minutes, or until the cheese begins to brown slightly.

• SERVES 4.

Tidbits

While I prefer the oven method of heating up the macaroni & cheese (since it adds a bit of browning and a slightly crunchy texture), you can also use your microwave oven to prepare the dish in a fraction of the time. Just be sure you freeze the macaroni & cheese in a mi-crowave-safe casserole dish following the recipe above. When you are ready to heat up the frozen cheesy awesomeness, simply cook it un-covered on high for 8 minutes, and then stir. Continue cooking on high for 2 to 3 more minutes, or until the macaroni & cheese is hot.

•   •   •   •

SUBWAY
BOURBON STREET GLAZE

☆　　✌　　💣　　✏　　☯　　✂　　☞

When you get right down to it, it's the sauce that makes this sandwich so good. If you take the Bourbon Street Glaze away from Subway's new Bourbon Street Chicken Sandwich, you end up with . . . a boring chicken sub. Once you've got this secret sauce cloned, you can drizzle it over your next boring chicken sub to experience the greatness that is one of Subway's most popular products.

²/₃ cup water
¹/₃ cup granulated sugar
1 tablespoon cornstarch
2 teaspoons Worcestershire sauce
2 teaspoons soy sauce
1 teaspoon ketchup
¹/₂ teaspoon salt
¹/₄ teaspoon garlic powder

¹/₄ teaspoon onion powder
¹/₈ teaspoon cayenne pepper
¹/₈ teaspoon ground black pepper
¹/₈ teaspoon ground cumin
¹/₈ teaspoon rubbed dried sage
2 tablespoons white vinegar
2 teaspoons lemon juice

1. Whisk together all the ingredients except the vinegar and lemon juice in a medium saucepan. Bring the mixture to a boil over medium heat, then reduce the heat and simmer for 1 minute, or until thick. Cool for 10 minutes.
2. Stir in the vinegar and lemon juice, then cover and chill for 1 hour before using as a sauce on grilled chicken sandwiches.

• MAKES ¾ CUP.

•　　•　　•　　•

SUBWAY
CHIPOTLE SOUTHWEST SAUCE

Everyone hip on Subway's sandwiches knows the key to cloning the flavor of many of the chain's top sellers is in re-creating the secret sauces. For example, Subway's Sweet Onion Chicken Teriyaki Sandwich is pretty bland without the Sweet Onion Sauce (page 239). And one of Subway's newest creations, the Chipotle Southwest Cheese Steak, is just a cheese steak sandwich without the Chipotle Southwest Sauce. Now, with this simple sauce clone, you can re-create the slightly sweet, mildly sour, and a little bit smoky sauce at home to take any of your sandwich creations on a trip to the spicy Southwest. But you don't have to stop at sandwiches. This sauce also makes an amazing dressing for a zesty Southwestern-style salad. You'll need to pick up some ground chipotle chile in the spice aisle of your market. McCormick makes good stuff.

¹/₂ cup mayonnaise	¹/₂ teaspoon water
2 teaspoons lime juice	¹/₄ teaspoon salt
1 teaspoon sugar	¹/₄ teaspoon garlic powder
1 teaspoon minced fresh cilantro	¹/₄ teaspoon ground chipotle chile
¹/₂ teaspoon paprika	pinch dried thyme
¹/₂ teaspoon white vinegar	pinch ground cumin

Combine all the ingredients in a small bowl. Cover and chill for at least 1 hour before using.

• MAKES ½ CUP.

SUBWAY
SWEET ONION SAUCE

☆ ✌ 💣 ✏ ☯ ✂ ☞

The Sweet Onion Chicken Teriyaki Sandwich is one of Subway's biggest new product rollouts in chain history. The sandwich is made with common ingredients: teriyaki-glazed chicken breast strips, onions, lettuce, tomatoes, green peppers, and olives. But what sets it apart from all other teriyaki chicken sandwiches is Subway's delicious Sweet Onion Sauce. You can ask for as much of the scrumptious sauce as you want on your custom-made sub at the huge sandwich chain, but you won't get any extra to take home, even if you offer to pay. Now you can add a clone version of the sauce to your home-built sandwich masterpieces whenever you want.

½ cup light corn syrup
1 tablespoon minced white onion
1 tablespoon red wine vinegar
2 teaspoons white vinegar
1 teaspoon balsamic vinegar
1 teaspoon brown sugar

1 teaspoon buttermilk powder
¼ teaspoon lemon juice
⅛ teaspoon poppy seeds
⅛ teaspoon salt
pinch cracked black pepper
pinch garlic powder

1. Combine all the ingredients in a small microwave-safe bowl.
2. Heat the mixture uncovered in the microwave for 1 to 1½ minutes on high until the mixture boils rapidly.
3. Whisk well, cover, and cool.

• MAKES ABOUT ⅔ CUP.

• • • •

TACO BELL
BAJA SAUCE

☆ ✌ 💣 ✒ ☻ ✂ ☞

This is the spicy sauce that you can order on your Gordita or Chalupa at Taco Bell, but you won't get much extra sauce—even if you order it on the side—to use later on all sorts of homemade Mexican masterpieces, from tacos to fajitas to breakfast burritos. But now, with this original TSR clone of the creamy sauce, you should have enough to hold you over for a while. You need a food processor to puree the vegetables, but don't expect to use all the puree. I've made the measurements for the puree larger than required so that your food processor will have something to grab on to. And by the way, this is a mayo-based sauce, so if you want to knock down the fat grams, use light mayonnaise in the recipe to make low-fat homemade Baja Sauce. You can't get that at Taco Bell!

*¹/₄ of a red bell pepper, seeded
  and coarsely chopped
I large jalapeño chile, chopped
  in half
2 tablespoons diced Spanish
  onion*

*I cup mayonnaise
I tablespoon white vinegar
¹/₄ teaspoon cracked black pepper
pinch garlic powder
pinch cumin*

1. Using a food processor, puree the peppers and onion.
2. Mix I cup mayonnaise and 4 teaspoons of the vegetable puree in a medium bowl. Add the remaining ingredients and mix well. Chill for several hours to let the flavors develop.

- MAKES I CUP.

TACO BELL
CHICKEN QUESADILLA

☆ ✌ 💣 ✏ ☯ ✂ ☞

Taco Bell takes the fast-food quesadilla into new territory with three different cheeses and a creamy jalapeño sauce, all of which you can now cheerfully re-create in the comfort of your warm kitchen. Gather up the crew, since this easy recipe will make four of the tasty tortilla treats.

CREAMY JALAPEÑO SAUCE

1/4 cup mayonnaise
2 teaspoons minced jalapeño
   slices (bottled)
2 teaspoons juice from jalapeño
   slices (from the bottle)
3/4 teaspoon granulated sugar

1/2 teaspoon paprika
1/2 teaspoon ground cumin
1/8 teaspoon cayenne pepper
1/8 teaspoon garlic powder
pinch salt

CHICKEN

4 chicken breast tenderloins
vegetable oil
salt and pepper
4 large (10-inch) flour tortillas

1 cup shredded cheddar cheese
1 cup shredded Monterey Jack
   cheese
2 slices American cheese

1. Prepare the creamy jalapeño sauce by combining all the ingredients in a small bowl. Cover and chill so the flavors develop. Stir occasionally.
2. Preheat your barbecue grill to medium heat.
3. Rub the chicken tenderloins with vegetable oil. Salt and pepper both sides of each tenderloin. Grill for 3 to 5 minutes per side. When the chicken is done, slice it very thin.

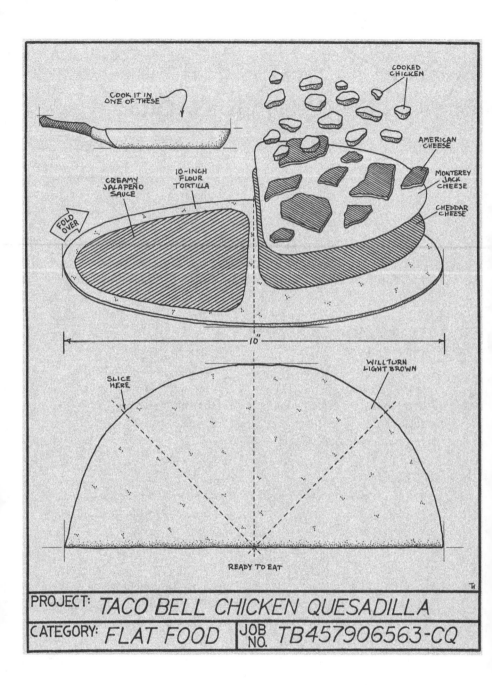

COOK IT IN
ONE OF THESE

COOKED
CHICKEN

AMERICAN
CHEESE

MONTEREY
JACK
CHEESE

CREAMY
JALAPEÑO
SAUCE

10-INCH
FLOUR
TORTILLA

CHEDDAR
CHEESE

FOLD
OVER

10"

SLICE
HERE

WILL TURN
LIGHT BROWN

READY TO EAT

PROJECT: *TACO BELL CHICKEN QUESADILLA*

CATEGORY: *FLAT FOOD*   JOB NO. *TB457906563-CQ*

4. When you are ready to build your quesadillas, preheat a 12-inch skillet over medium-low heat.
5. When the pan is hot, lay one tortilla in the pan. Arrange about ¼ cup of shredded cheddar cheese and ¼ cup of shredded Jack cheese on half the tortilla. Tear up half a slice of American cheese and arrange it on the other cheeses.
6. Arrange about ¼ cup of sliced chicken over the cheese.
7. Spread about 1 tablespoon of jalapeño sauce over the tortilla on the half with no ingredients on it.
8. Fold the sauced-covered half of the tortilla over onto the ingredients on the other half and press down with a spatula. Cook for about 1 minute, then turn the quesadilla over and cook for a couple more minutes, or until the cheese inside is melted. Slice into 4 pieces and serve hot. Repeat with the remaining ingredients.

- MAKES 4 QUESADILLAS.

Tidbits

Look for bottled jalapeño slices. They are sometimes called "nacho slices" and can be found near the pickles in your supermarket.

•   •   •   •

TACO BELL
MILD BORDER SAUCE

☆   ✌   💣   ✏   ☯   ✂   ☞

If you like the flavor of Taco Bell's sauce without the burn, this is the sauce to clone. It used to be that you could get this sauce only in the little blister packs from Taco Bell restaurants, but now the chain has partnered with Kraft Foods to sell the stuff in 7.5-ounce bottles in supermarkets. For the record, those bottles of hot sauce will set you back around $1.59 at the store, while the 6-ounce can of tomato paste required for this recipe is only 59 cents—and you end up with more than three times the amount of sauce!

3 cups water	4 teaspoons chili powder
2 teaspoons cornstarch	2 teaspoons salt
one 6-ounce can tomato paste	1 teaspoon cayenne pepper
3 tablespoons white vinegar	

1. Dissolve the cornstarch in the water in a medium saucepan.
2. Add the remaining ingredients and stir well. Bring the mixture to a boil over medium heat, then reduce the heat and simmer for 5 minutes. Turn off the heat and cover the sauce until it has cooled. Store the sauce in a covered container in your refrigerator.

• MAKES 3 CUPS (24 OUNCES).

• • • •

WEIGHT WATCHERS SMART ONES BANANA MUFFINS

This easy muffin clone is modeled after the low-fat product found in the freezer section of your market from one of the first brands to make low-fat food hip and tasty. Muffins are notorious for their high fat content, but in this recipe mashed banana adds flavor and moistness to the muffins so that less fat is needed. Now you can satisfy a muffin craving without worrying about fat grams.

1 ¹/₄ cups granulated sugar	¹/₂ teaspoon banana flavoring
¹/₂ cup mashed banana	¹/₄ teaspoon lemon extract
¹/₂ cup milk	1 ¹/₂ cups all-purpose flour
¹/₃ cup buttermilk	¹/₂ teaspoon baking soda
1 tablespoon egg substitute	¹/₂ teaspoon baking powder
1 teaspoon vegetable oil	³/₄ teaspoon salt
1 teaspoon vanilla extract	

1. Preheat the oven to 350 degrees F.
2. Combine the sugar, banana, milk, buttermilk, egg substitute, oil, vanilla, banana flavoring, and lemon extract in a large bowl. Mix well with an electric mixer on high speed.
3. In a medium bowl, combine the flour, baking soda, baking powder, and salt.
4. Mix the dry ingredients into the wet ingredients with the electric mixer.

5. Pour the batter into the muffin cups of a muffin tin until each cup is about ⅔ full.
6. Bake for 25 to 30 minutes, or until the muffins turn light brown on top.

• Makes 12 muffins.

• • • •

WENDY'S
GARDEN SENSATIONS
MANDARIN CHICKEN SALAD

☆   ✌   💣   ✏   ☯   ✂   ☞

Of the four salads on Wendy's Garden Sensations menu, this is the one that elicited all the cloning requests here at TSR Central. It's the sesame dressing that everyone's nuts about. The formula below gives you a nice 1½ cups of the delicious stuff so it'll fit perfectly into a standard dressing cruet. Once you've got your dressing made, building the rest of the salad is a breeze.

SESAME DRESSING

½ cup corn syrup
3 tablespoons white vinegar
2 tablespoons pineapple juice
4 teaspoons granulated sugar
1 tablespoon light brown sugar
1 tablespoon rice wine vinegar
1 tablespoon soy sauce
1 teaspoon sesame oil

¼ teaspoon ground mustard
¼ teaspoon ground ginger
⅛ teaspoon salt
⅛ teaspoon paprika
pinch garlic powder
pinch ground black pepper
½ cup vegetable oil
½ teaspoon sesame seeds

4 chicken breast fillets
vegetable oil
salt and pepper
1 large head iceberg lettuce, chopped
4 cups chopped red leaf lettuce

1⅓ cups canned mandarin orange wedges
1 cup rice noodles (or chow mein noodles)
1 cup roasted sliced almonds

1. Prepare the dressing by combining all the dressing ingredients except the vegetable oil and sesame seeds in a blender on high speed. Slowly add the oil to mixture through the hole in the lid—it will thicken and create an emulsion. Add the sesame seeds and blend for just a couple of seconds. Pour the dressing into a container (such as a dressing cruet), cover, and chill until needed.
2. Rub each chicken breast fillet with oil, then lightly salt and pepper each piece. Grill on medium-high heat until done. Chill the chicken breasts in your refrigerator until cold.
3. When the chicken is cold, build each salad by first arranging about 4 cups of iceberg lettuce in the bottom of a large salad bowl or on a plate.
4. Arrange a cup of red leaf lettuce on the iceberg lettuce.
5. Dice each chicken breast into bite-size pieces and sprinkle the pieces from each one over each salad.
6. Arrange about ⅓ cup of mandarin orange wedges on each salad.
7. Next, sprinkle about ¼ cup of rice noodles and ¼ cup of roasted sliced almonds on top of each salad.
8. Add the desired amount of sesame dressing and serve.

• MAKES 4 LARGE SALADS.

•   •   •   •

WENDY'S WILD MOUNTAIN BACON CHEESEBURGER

☆　✌　💣　✏　☯　✗　☞

The secret to duplicating the taste of this great Wendy's burger comes down to re-creating the spicy Southwestern pepper sauce. And, if you want to stay true to the original burger, you'll have to get yourself some sliced yellow and white Colby Jack cheese. Look for the marbled cheese in the deli section—I used Tillamook brand. Cook up some bacon, slap it all together, and you'll have one of the best homemade hamburgers on the planet.

SOUTHWESTERN PEPPER SAUCE

$1/3$ cup mayonnaise
$3/4$ teaspoon paprika
$1/4$ teaspoon ground cumin
$1/4$ teaspoon minced garlic
$1/4$ teaspoon lemon juice

$1/8$ teaspoon cayenne pepper
$1/8$ teaspoon dried oregano
pinch salt
pinch granulated sugar

$3 1/4$ ounces ground beef
1 kaiser bun (no seeds)
salt and pepper
1 slice Colby Jack cheese

2 slices cooked bacon
1 leaf iceberg lettuce
2 tomato slices
2 red onion rings

1. Make the Southwestern pepper sauce by combining all the ingredients in a small bowl. Cover and chill the sauce until it's needed.
2. Form the ground beef on wax paper into a square patty that is slightly bigger than the diameter of the bun. Put the patty into

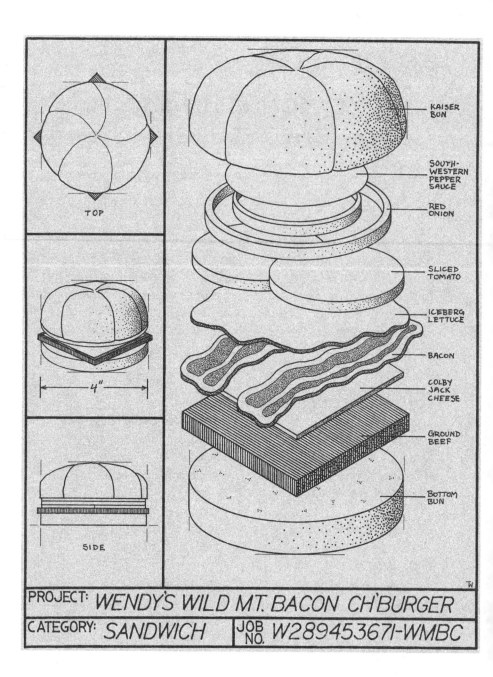

TOP

4"

SIDE

KAISER BUN

SOUTH-WESTERN PEPPER SAUCE

RED ONION

SLICED TOMATO

ICEBERG LETTUCE

BACON

COLBY JACK CHEESE

GROUND BEEF

BOTTOM BUN

PROJECT: *WENDY'S WILD MT. BACON CH'BURGER*

CATEGORY: *SANDWICH*   **JOB NO.** *W28945367I-WMBC*

the freezer for at least 30 minutes so that it will firm up. This prevents the ground beef from falling apart as it cooks.

3. When you're ready to make the burger, heat up a large skillet or griddle pan over medium heat. Brown the faces of the kaiser bun on the hot pan. When the faces of the bun are lightly browned, use the pan to cook the beef patty. Add a sprinkle of salt and pepper to the meat, and then cook it for 2 to 3 minutes per side, or until done.

4. Assemble the burger by positioning the patty on the bottom bun half. Place the slice of cheese on the beef, followed by the slices of cooked bacon. Place the lettuce leaf on the bacon, than add the tomato slices and 2 rings that have been separated from 1 slice of a red onion. Spread about 1 tablespoon of Southwestern sauce on the face of the top bun. Flip the top over onto the rest of the sandwich and mow down.

• MAKES 1 SANDWICH.

Tidbits

Wendy's also serves this sandwich with two patties. If you like your burgers thick, just add another beef patty onto the first one (on top of the cheese), followed by another slice of Colby Jack.

•   •   •   •

YONAH SCHIMMEL
LOW-FAT NEW YORK CITY
KNISH

☆   ✌   💣   ✏   ☯   ✂   ☞

Here's a recipe that comes from a challenge issued by the *New York Daily News*. They wanted to find out if a West Coast dude could duplicate the taste of an authentic New York City knish. But, mind you, not just any knish. This knish comes from one of the oldest knisheries in the Big Apple, a place that also takes pride in the low fat content of its knishes as opposed to the popular deep-fried variety. When I tasted the famous Yonah Schimmel knish (the first knish I had ever sampled), I realized that not only could a simple clone recipe be created, but that the fat gram count could come in even lower. The *Daily News* even went so far as to have a lab analyze the fat content of not only the original knish and the clone but also the fat grams in a street vendor knish and a supermarket knish, just for comparison. The lab results are listed following the recipe.

6 medium russet potatoes
5 tablespoons reduced-fat butter
³/₄ cup minced white onion (about ¹/₄ of an onion)

¹/₂ cup fat-free chicken broth
1 teaspoon salt
¹/₄ teaspoon ground black pepper

OPTIONAL

1 tablespoon chopped chives
¹/₂ teaspoon red pepper flakes

12 sheets phyllo dough

1. Peel and quarter the potatoes, then transfer them to a large saucepan and cover with water. Bring to a boil over medium heat

and boil for 25 minutes, or until a knife stuck in a potato quarter encounters no resistance. Strain the water from the potatoes and then mash them in a large bowl.

2. Sauté the onion in 2 tablespoons butter over medium-low heat for about 5 minutes, or until translucent but not brown. Add the onion to the mashed potatoes, along with the broth, salt, pepper, and chives and/or red pepper flakes, if desired. Melt an additional 1 tablespoon butter (in your microwave is easiest) and add that to the potatoes as well. Stir to combine.

3. Melt the remaining 2 tablespoons butter in a small bowl in the microwave. Preheat the oven to 375 degrees F.

4. Slice in half a stack of 3 sheets of phyllo dough (roll up all remaining sheets so that they do not dry out). Measure 1 cup of potato mixture and roll it into a ball with your hands. Place the ball into the center of the phyllo, then bring up the dough and wrap it around the potato filling. Brush the dough with melted butter to keep it sealed around the potato filling, and place the knish onto a baking sheet. Repeat with the remaining ingredients—you should have 8 knishes—and bake for 40 to 45 minutes, or until the knishes are nicely browned.

• MAKES 8 KNISHES.

How They Stack Up

Top Secret Recipes knish—Price: 40 cents, Weight: 6.75 ounces, Fat: 3.63 grams

Yonah Schimmel knish—Price: $1.50, Weight: 11.27 ounces, Fat: 7.01 grams

Street vendor knish—Price: $1, Weight: 4.35 ounces, Fat: 4.53 grams

Supermarket knish—Price $1.50, Weight: 9.89 ounces, Fat: 11.27 grams

• • • •

TRADEMARKS

Arby's and Horsey Sauce are registered trademarks of Arby's IP Holder Trust.

Baja Fresh is a registered trademark of Fresh Enterprises.

Bisquick and Chex Mix are registered trademarks of General Mills.

Boston Market is a registered trademark of Boston Market Corporation.

Budweiser is a registered trademark of Anheuser-Busch, Inc.

Burger King is a registered trademark of Burger King Brands, Inc.

Carl's Jr. and Six Dollar Burger are registered trademarks of Carl Karcher Enterprises, Inc.

Carnegie Deli is a registered trademark of Carnegie Deli, Inc.

Chick-fil-A is a registered trademark of CFA Properties, Inc.

Chipotle is a registered trademark of Chipotle Mexican Grill, Inc.

Cliff & Buster is a registered trademark of Cliff & Buster, Inc.

Coca-Cola and Blāk are registered trademarks of The Coca-Cola Company.

Crunch 'n Munch, Lincoln Snacks, and Poppycock are registered trademarks of ConAgra Foods, Inc.

Dairy Queen, MooLatté, and Orange Julius are registered trademarks of International Dairy Queen, Inc.

Del Taco is a registered trademark of Del Taco LLC.

Duncan Hines and Moist Deluxe are registered trademarks of Pinnacle Foods Group, Inc.

Dunkin' Donuts and Coolatta are registered trademarks of Dunkin' Brands, Inc.

Einstein Bros. is a registered trademark of Einstein Noah Restaurant Group, Inc.

El Pollo Loco is a registered trademark of El Pollo Loco, Inc.

Famous Amos is a registered trademark of Kellogg NA Co.

Fritos is a registered trademark of Frito-Lay North America, Inc.

Heinz, Weight Watchers, and Smart Ones are registered trademarks of H. J. Heinz Company.

Hellmann's/Best Foods, Ragú, and Spatini are registered trademarks of Unilever.

Hidden Valley and The Original Ranch are registered trademarks of The Clorox Company.

Jack in the Box is a registered trademark of Jack in the Box, Inc.

Jacquin's Peppermint Schnapps is a registered trademark of Charles Jacquin et Cie., Inc.

Jason's Deli is a registered trademark of Jason's Deli.

Jimmy Dean is a registered trademark of Sara Lee Corporation.

KFC, Taco Bell, and Border Sauce are registered trademarks of Yum! Brands.

Kozy Shack is a registered trademark of Kozy Shack, Inc.

Kraft and Miracle Whip are registered trademarks of Kraft Foods, Inc.

Krispy Kreme is a registered trademark of Krispy Kreme Doughnuts, Inc.

Lawry's is a registered trademark of Lawry's Foods, Inc.

Lipton and Brisk are registered trademarks of Lipton Tea, Inc.

Maid-Rite is a registered trademark of Maid-Rite Corporation.

Mars and Munch are registered trademarks of Mars, Incorporated and its Affiliates.

Mauna Loa and Kona Coffee Glazed are registered trademarks of The Hershey Company.

McDonald's is a registered trademark of McDonald's Corporation.

Mrs. Fields is a registered trademark of Mrs. Fields, Inc.

No Pudge! is a registered trademark of No Pudge Fat Free Brownies.

Old Bay is a registered trademark of McCormick & Co., Inc.

Pals and Sauce Burger are registered trademarks of Pal's Sudden Service, Inc.

Panera Bread is a registered trademark of Panera Bread, Inc.

Pepperidge Farm is a registered trademark of Pepperidge Farm, Incorporated.

Popeyes and Cajun Sparkle are registered trademarks of Popeyes Louisiana Kitchen, AFC Enterprises, Inc.

Rondelé is a registered trademark of Lactalis Deli, Inc.

Sabra is a registered trademark of Sabra Dipping Co. LLC.

Skyline is a registered trademark of Skyline Chili, Inc.

Sonic Drive-In is a registered trademark of America's Drive-In Brand Properties LLC.

Starbucks and Frappuccino are registered trademarks of Starbucks Corporation.

Stouffer's is a registered trademark of Nestlé USA, Inc.

Subway is a registered trademark of Doctor's Associates, Inc.

Tabasco is a registered trademark of McIlhenny Company.

Wendy's and Garden Sensations are registered trademarks of Wendy's International, Inc.

INDEX

Arby's Horsey Sauce, 1
Avocado Salsa, El Pollo Loco, 56

Bagel
    Cranberry Walnut, Panera Bread,
        143–45
    Santa Fe Egg Sandwich, Einstein
        Bros. Bagels, 54–55
Baja Fresh Salsa Baja, 2–3
Baja Sauce, Taco Bell, 240
Baking Mix, Bisquick Original All-
    Purpose, 4–5
Banana
    Julius, Orange Julius, 136
    Muffins, Smart Ones, Weight
        Watchers, 245–46
    Strawberry Classic Smoothie,
        Orange Julius, 137–38
Barbacoa Burrito, Chipotle Mexican
    Grill, 33–37
Barbecue Sauce, Honey Roasted,
    Chick-fil-A, 27–28
BBQ Black Beans, El Pollo Loco, 57–58
Beans
    BBQ Black, El Pollo Loco, 57–58
    Hot Dip, Fritos, 63
    Pinto, Chipotle Mexican Grill, 34
    Red & Rice, Popeyes, 161–63
Beef, ground
    Loose Meat Sandwich, Maid-Rite,
        102–5
    Ragú Pasta Sauce, 164–65
    See also Burger

Beer, Budweiser Chelada, 13
Biscotti, Vanilla Almond, Starbucks, 231–33
Biscuits
    Baking Mix, Bisquick Original All-
        Purpose, 4–5
    Buttermilk, Popeyes, 155–57
Bisquick Original All-Purpose Baking
    Mix, 4–5
Black Beans, BBQ, El Pollo Loco, 57–58
Boston Market
    Butternut Squash, 6–7
    Garlic Dill New Potatoes, 8–10
    Sweet Potato Casserole, 11–12
Bourbon Street Glaze, Subway, 237
Breakfast Sausage, Jimmy Dean, 75–76
Brisk Iced Tea, Lipton, 96
Broccoli Cheddar Soup, Panera Bread,
    141–42
Brownies
    No Pudge! Original Fat Free Fudge
        Brownie Mix, 130–32
    Peppermint, Starbucks, 217–19
Budweiser Chelada, 13
Buns, Cinnamon Melts, McDonald's,
    115–18
Burger
    Hickory, Sonic Drive-In, 178–79
    Jalapeño, Sonic Drive-In, 180–82
    Sauce, Pal's, 139–40
    Six Dollar, Carl's Jr., 18–20
    Sonic, Sonic Drive-In, 175–77
    Wild Mountain Bacon
        Cheeseburger, Wendy's, 249–51

Burger King
   Onion Rings, 14–16
   Onion Ring Sauce, Zesty, 17
Burrito, Barbacoa, Chipotle Mexican
   Grill, 33–37
Buttermilk Biscuits, Popeyes, 155–57
Butternut Squash, Boston Market, 6–7

Cajun Gravy, Popeyes, 158–59
Cajun Honey Wings, KFC, 77–79
Cajun Sparkle, Popeyes, 160
Cake
   Carrot, Starbucks, 203–4
   Cheesecake, New York City Classic,
      Carnegie Deli, 21–23
   Coffee, Starbucks, 205–7
   Cranberry Bliss Bar, Starbucks,
      208–10
   Lemon Loaf, Starbucks, 211–13
   Pumpkin Bread, Starbucks, 220–22
   Yellow Cake Mix, Moist Deluxe,
      Duncan Hines, 50–51
Candied Nuts. See Nuts
Candy bar, Munch Bar, Mars, 106–8
Caramel Macchiato, Starbucks, 193–94
Carl's Jr., Six Dollar Burger, 18–20
Carnegie Deli, New York City
   Cheesecake, 21–23
Carrot and Raisin Salad, Chick-fil-A,
   29–30
Carrot Cake, Starbucks, 203–4
Cheesecake, New York City Classic,
   Carnegie Deli, 21–23
Cheese spread, Garlic & Herbs,
   Rondelé, 166–67
Chelada, Budweiser, 13
Chex Mix, Bold Party Blend, 24–26
Chicken
   Cajun Honey Wings, KFC, 77–79
   Mandarin Chicken Salad, Wendy's,
      247–48
   Mexican Chicken Chili, Soup Nazi,
      189–90
   Pot Pie, KFC, 80–83
   Quesadilla, Taco Bell, 241–43

Chick-fil-A
   Carrot and Raisin Salad, 29–30
   Honey Roasted BBQ Sauce, 27–28
Chili
   Mexican Chicken Chili, Soup Nazi,
      189–90
   Skyline, 170–71
Chili Sauce, Heinz Premium, 64–65
Chipotle Mexican Grill
   Barbacoa Burrito, 33–37
   Chipotle-Honey Vinaigrette, 31–32
   Cilantro-Lime Rice, 34
   Pico De Gallo, 34
   Pinto Beans, 34
Chipotle Southwest Sauce, Subway,
   238
Chocolate Chip Cookies, Famous
   Amos, 60–62
Cilantro
   Cilantro-Lime Rice, Chipotle
      Mexican Grill, 34
   Dressing, Creamy, El Pollo Loco, 59
Cinnamon Melts, McDonald's, 115–18
Cliff & Buster Coconut Macaroons,
   38–40
Coca-Cola Blāk, 41–43
Coconut Macaroons, Cliff & Buster,
   38–40
Coffee Cake, Starbucks, 205–7
Coffee drinks
   Caramel Macchiato, Starbucks,
      193–94
   Coca-Cola, Blāk, 41–43
   Coffee Coolatta, Dunkin' Donuts,
      52–53
   Frappuccino (bottled version),
      Starbucks, 195–96
   Gingerbread Latte, Starbucks,
      197–98
   Mocha Coconut Frappuccino,
      Starbucks, 201–2
   MooLatté, Dairy Queen, 45–46
   Vanilla Iced, McDonald's, 113–14
Cookies
   Chocolate Chip, Famous Amos, 60–62

Coconut Macaroons, Cliff & Buster, 38–40

Cranberry White Chocolate, Mrs. Fields, 124–26

Snickerdoodle, Soft Baked, Pepperidge Farm, 152–54

Vanilla Almond Biscotti, Starbucks, 231–33

Crab Bisque, Soup Nazi, 183–84

Cranberry
Bliss Bar, Starbucks, 208–10
Walnut Bagel, Panera Bread, 143–45
White Chocolate Cookies, Mrs. Fields, 124–26

Cream of Sweet Potato Soup, Soup Nazi, 185–86

Creamy Cilantro Dressing, El Pollo Loco, 59

Creamy Jalapeño Sauce, Taco Bell, 241–43

Creamy Liqueur Fruit Dipping Sauce, Jason's, 74

Crispy Fish Taco, Del Taco, 47–49

Crunch 'n Munch, Buttery Toffee Popcorn with Peanuts, 43–44

Dairy Queen MooLatté, 45–46

Del Taco
Crispy Fish Taco, 47–49
Secret Sauce, 47, 49

Diet Green Tea with Citrus, Lipton, 97–98

Dips
Hot Bean, Fritos, 63
Hummus, Sabra, 168–69
Liqueur Fruit Dipping Sauce, Creamy, Jason's, 74

Doughnuts, Glazed, Original, Krispy Kreme, 89–93

Dressing
Chipotle-Honey Vinaigrette, 31–32
Cilantro, Creamy, El Pollo Loco, 59
Mayonnaise, Hellmann's/Best Foods, 66–68
Miracle Whip, Kraft, 87–88

Ranch, Hidden Valley Original, 69–70
Sesame, Wendy's, 247–48

Drinks
Banana Julius, Orange Julius, 136
Budweiser Chelada, 13
Hot Chocolate, Starbucks, 199–200
Peppermint Schnapps, Jacquin's, 73
Strawberry-Banana Classic Smoothie, Orange Julius, 137–38
See also Coffee drinks; Shakes; Tea

Duncan Hines Moist Deluxe Yellow Cake Mix, 50–51

Dunkin' Donuts, Coffee Coolatta, 52–53

Egg
Santa Fe Egg Sandwich, Einstein Bros. Bagels, 54–55
Spinach Artichoke Baked Egg Soufflé, Panera Bread, 148–51

Einstein Bros. Bagels Santa Fe Egg Sandwich, 54–55

El Pollo Loco
Avocado Salsa, 56
BBQ Black Beans, 57–58
Cilantro Dressing, Creamy, 59

Famous Amos Chocolate Chip Cookies, 60–62

Fat Free Fudge Brownie Mix, Original, No Pudge! 130–32

Fish, Crispy Taco, Del Taco, 47–49

Frappuccino
bottled version, Starbucks, 195–96
Mocha Coconut, Starbucks, 201–2

French Onion Soup, Panera Bread, 146–47

Fritos Hot Bean Dip, 63

Fruit
Liqueur Dipping Sauce, Creamy, Jason's, 74
& Walnut Salad, McDonalds, 119–20

Garlic & Herbs Cheese Spread, Rondelé, 166–67

Garlic Dill New Potatoes, Boston
    Market, 8–10
Gingerbread Latte, Starbucks, 197–98
Glaze, Bourbon Street, Subway, 237
Gravy, Cajun, Popeyes, 158–59

Hamburger. See Burger
Heinz Premium Chili Sauce, 64–65
Hellmann's/Best Foods Mayonnaise,
    66–68
Hickory Burger, Sonic Drive-In, 178–79
Hidden Valley Original Ranch Dressing,
    69–70
Honey Mustard, Tangy, McDonald's, 121
Honey Roasted BBQ Sauce, Chick-fil-
    A, 27–28
Horseradish Sauce, Horsey Sauce,
    Arby's, 1
Horsey Sauce, Arby's, 1
Hot Bean Dip, Fritos, 63
Hot Chocolate, Starbucks, 199–200
Hummus, Sabra, 168–69

Indian Mulligatwany, Soup Nazi, 187–88

Jack in the Box Pumpkin Pie Shake,
    71–72
Jacquin's Peppermint Schnapps, 73
Jalapeño Burger, Sonic Drive-In, 180–82
Jalapeño Sauce, Creamy, Taco Bell,
    241–43
Jason's Deli Creamy Liqueur Fruit
    Dipping Sauce, 74
Jimmy Dean Breakfast Sausage,
    75–76

KFC
    Cajun Honey Wings, 77–79
    Chicken Pot Pie, 80–83
Knish, Low-Fat New York City, Yonah
    Schimmel, 252–53
Kozy Shack Rice Pudding, 84–86
Kraft Miracle Whip, 87–88
Krispy Kreme, Original Glazed
    Doughnuts, 89–93

Lawry's Red Pepper Seasoned Salt,
    94–95
Lemon Loaf, Starbucks, 211–13
Lincoln Snacks Poppycock, 99–101
Lipton
    Brisk Iced Tea, 96
    Diet Green Tea with Citrus, 97–98
Liqueur Fruit Dipping Sauce, Creamy,
    Jason's, 74
Lobster, McLobster Sandwich,
    McDonald's, 122–23
Loose Meat Sandwich, Maid-Rite,
    102–5
Low-Fat New York City Knish, Yonah
    Schimmel, 252–53

Macadamia nuts, Mauna Loa Kona
    Coffee Glazed, 109–11
Macaroni & Cheese, Stouffer's, 234–36
McDonald's
    Cinnamon Melts, 115–18
    Fruit & Walnut Salad, 119–20
    McLobster Sandwich, 122–23
    Sweet Tea, 112
    Tangy Honey Mustard, 121
    Vanilla Iced Coffee, 113–14
Maid-Rite Loose Meat Sandwich,
    102–5
Mandarin Chicken Salad, Wendy's,
    247–48
Maple Oat Nut Scone, Starbucks,
    214–16
Mars Munch Bar, 106–8
Mauna Loa Kona Coffee Glazed
    Macadamias, 109–11
Mayonnaise, Hellmann's/Best Foods,
    66–68
Mexican Chicken Chili, Soup Nazi,
    189–90
Mild Border Sauce, Taco Bell, 244
Miracle Whip, Kraft, 87–88
Mocha Coconut Frappuccino,
    Starbucks, 201–2
MooLatté, Dairy Queen, 45–46
Mrs. Fields

Cranberry White Chocolate
    Cookies, 124–26
Pumpkin Harvest Cookies, 127–29
Muffin
    Banana, Smart Ones, Weight
        Watchers, 245–46
    Pumpkin Cream Cheese, Starbucks,
        223–26
Munch Bar, Mars, 106–8
Mustard, Tangy Honey, McDonald's, 121

No Pudge! Original Fat Free Fudge
    Brownie Mix, 130–32
Nuts
    Candied, Nuts 4 Nuts, 133–34
    Candied Walnuts, in Fruit and Walnut
        Salad, McDonald's, 119–20
    Macadamia, Mauna Loa Kona Coffee
        Glazed, 109–11
    Munch Bar, Mars, 106–8
Nuts 4 Nuts, Candied Nuts, 133–34

Old Bay Seasoning, 135
Onion
    Rings, Burger King, 14–16
    Ring Sauce, Burger King, 17
    Sauce, Sweet, Subway, 239
Orange Julius
    Banana Julius, 136
    Orange Julius, 136
    Strawberry-Banana Classic Smoothie,
        137–38

Pal's Sauce Burger, 139–40
Pancakes, Baking Mix, Bisquick Original
    All-Purpose, 4–5
Panera Bread
    Broccoli Cheddar Soup, 141–42
    Cranberry Walnut Bagel, 143–45
    French Onion Soup, 146–47
    Spinach Artichoke Baked Egg
        Soufflé, 148–51
Party Blend, Bold, Chex Mix, 24–26
Pasta sauces
    Ragú, 164–65

Spaghetti Mix, Spatini, 191–92
Peanut Butter Fudge Shake, Sonic
    Drive-In, 172
Peanut Butter Shake, Sonic Drive-In, 172
Pepperidge Farm Soft Baked
    Snickerdoodle Cookies, 152–54
Peppermint Brownie, Starbucks, 217–19
Peppermint Schnapps, Jacquin's, 73
Pico De Gallo, Chipotle Mexican Grill,
    34
Pinto Beans, Chipotle Mexican Grill, 34
Popcorn
    Buttery Toffee with Peanuts, Crunch
        'n Munch, 43–44
    Poppycock, Lincoln Snacks, 99–101
Popeyes
    Buttermilk Biscuits, 155–57
    Cajun Gravy, 158–59
    Cajun Sparkle, 160
    Red Beans & Rice, 161–63
Poppycock, Lincoln Snacks, 99–101
Potatoes, Garlic Dill New, Boston
    Market, 8–10
Pot Pie, Chicken, KFC, 80–83
Pudding, Rice, Kozy Shack, 84–86
Pumpkin
    Bread, Starbucks, 220–22
    Cream Cheese Muffin, Starbucks,
        223–26
    Harvest Cookies, Mrs. Fields, 127–29
    Pie Shake, Jack in the Box, 71–72
    Scone, Starbucks, 227–30

Quesadilla, Chicken, Taco Bell, 241–43

Ragú Pasta Sauces, 164–65
Ranch Dressing, Hidden Valley Original,
    69–70
Red Beans & Rice, Popeyes, 161–63
Red Pepper Seasoned Salt, Lawry's, 94–95
Rice
    Cilantro-Lime, Chipotle Mexican
        Grill, 34
    Pudding, Kozy Shack, 84–86
    Red Beans &, Popeyes, 161–63

Rondelé, Garlic & Herbs Cheese
    Spread, 166–67

Sabra Hummus, 168–69
Salad
    Carrot and Raisin, Chick-fil-A, 29–30
    Fruit & Walnut, McDonald's, 119–20
    Mandarin Chicken, Wendy's, 247–48
Salad dressing. See Dressing
Salsa
    Avocado, El Pollo Loco, 56
    Baja, Baja Fresh, 2–3
    Del Taco, 47, 49
Salt, Red Pepper Seasoned, Lawry's,
    94–95
Sandwich
    Loose Meat, Maid-Rite, 102–5
    McLobster, McDonald's, 122–23
    Santa Fe Egg, Einstein Bros. Bagels,
    54–55
Santa Fe Egg Sandwich, Einstein Bros.
    Bagels, 54–55
Sauce
    Baja, Taco Bell, 240
    Border, Mild, Taco Bell, 244
    Bourbon Street Glaze, Subway, 237
    Cajun Honey, KFC, 77–79
    Chili, Heinz Premium, 64–65
    Chipotle Southwest, Subway, 238
    Honey Roasted BBQ, Chick-fil-A,
    27–28
    Horsey, Arby's, 1
    Jalapeño, Creamy, Taco Bell, 241–43
    Liqueur Fruit Dipping, Creamy,
    Jason's, 74
    Onion Ring, Zesty, Burger King, 17
    Pico De Gallo, Chipotle Mexican
    Grill, 34
    Ragú Pasta, 164–65
    Salsa Baja, Baja Fresh, 2–3
    Secret, Del Taco, 47, 49
    Southwestern Pepper, Wendy's,
    249–51
    Spaghetti Mix, Spatini, 191–92
    Sweet Onion, Subway, 239

Sauce Burger, Pal's, 139–40
Sausage, Breakfast, Jimmy Dean, 75–76
Scone
    Maple Oat Nut, Starbucks, 214–16
    Pumpkin, Starbucks, 227–30
Seasoning and spices
    Cajun Sparkle, Popeyes, 160
    Chili Sauce, Heinz Premium, 64–65
    Honey Mustard, Tangy, McDonald's,
    121
    Old Bay, 135
    Red Pepper Seasoned Salt, Lawry's,
    94–95
Secret Sauce, Del Taco, 47, 49
Sesame Dressing, Wendy's, 247–48
Shakes
    Peanut Butter, Sonic Drive-In, 172
    Peanut Butter Fudge, Sonic Drive-In,
    172
    Pumpkin Pie, Jack in the Box, 71–72
    Strawberry Cheesecake, Sonic
    Drive-In, 173–74
Skyline Chili, 170–71
Smoothie, Strawberry-Banana Classic,
    Orange Julius, 137–38
Snack mix
    Bold Party Blend, Chex Mix, 24–26
    popcorn-based. See Popcorn
Snickerdoodle Cookies, Soft Baked,
    Pepperidge Farm, 152–54
Sonic Drive-In
    Hickory Burger, 178–79
    Jalapeño Burger, 180–82
    Peanut Butter Fudge Shake, 172
    Peanut Butter Shake, 172
    Sonic Burger, 175–77
    Strawberry Cheesecake Shake,
    173–74
Soup
    Broccoli Cheddar, Panera Bread,
    141–42
    Crab Bisque, Soup Nazi, 183–84
    Cream of Sweet Potato, Soup Nazi,
    185–86
    French Onion, Panera Bread, 146–47

Indian Mulligatwany, Soup Nazi, 187–88
Mexican Chicken Chili, Soup Nazi,
    189–90
Soup Kitchen International (Soup Nazi)
    Crab Bisque, 183–84
    Cream of Sweet Potato Soup,
        185–86
    Indian Mulligatwany, 187–88
    Mexican Chicken Chili, 189–90
Soup Nazi. See Soup Kitchen
    International (Soup Nazi)
Southwestern Pepper Sauce, Wendy's,
    249–51
Spaghetti Sauce Mix, Spatini, 191–92
Spatini Spaghetti Sauce Mix, 191–92
Spinach Artichoke Baked Egg Soufflé,
    Panera Bread, 148–51
Spread, Garlic & Herbs Cheese,
    Rondelé, 166–67
Squash, Butternut, Boston Market, 6–7
Starbucks
    Caramel Macchiato, 193–94
    Carrot Cake, 203–4
    Coffee Cake, 205–7
    Cranberry Bliss Bar, 208–10
    Frappuccino (bottled version),
        195–95
    Gingerbread Latte, 197–98
    Hot Chocolate, 199–200
    Lemon Loaf, 211–13
    Maple Oat Nut Scone, 214–16
    Mocha Coconut Frappuccino, 201–2
    Peppermint Brownie, 217–19
    Pumpkin Bread, 220–22
    Pumpkin Cream Cheese Muffin,
        223–26
    Pumpkin Scone, 227–30
    Vanilla Almond Biscotti, 231–33
Stouffer's Macaroni & Cheese, 234–36
Strawberry-Banana Classic Smoothie,
    Orange Julius, 137–38
Subway
    Bourbon Street Glaze, 237
    Chipotle Southwest Sauce, 238
    Sweet Onion Sauce, 239

Sweet Onion Sauce, Subway, 239
Sweet Potato Casserole, Boston
    Market, 11–12
Sweet Potato Soup, Cream of, Soup
    Kitchen International, 185–86

Taco, Crispy Fish, Del Taco, 47–49
Taco Bell
    Baja Sauce, 240
    Chicken Quesadilla, 241–43
    Jalapeño Sauce, Creamy, 241–43
    Mild Border Sauce, 244
Tea
    Brisk Iced, Lipton, 96
    Diet Green with Citrus, Lipton,
        97–98
    Sweet, McDonald's, 112
Tomato sauce, Ragú, 164–65

Vanilla Almond Biscotti, Starbucks,
    231–33
    Vanilla Iced Coffee, McDonald's,
        113–14
    Vegetables. See specific vegetables
    Vinaigrette, Chipotle-Honey,
        Chipotle Mexican Grill, 31–32

Waffles, Baking Mix, Bisquick Original
    All-Purpose, 4–5
Weight Watchers Smart Ones Banana
    Muffins, 245–46
Wendy's
    Mandarin Chicken Salad, 247–48
    Sesame Dressing, 247–48
    Southwestern Pepper Sauce,
        249–51
    Wild Mountain Bacon
        Cheeseburger, 249–51
Wild Mountain Bacon Cheeseburger,
    Wendy's, 249–51

Yellow Cake Mix, Moist Deluxe,
    Duncan Hines, 50–51
Yonah Schimmel Low-Fat New York
    City Knish, 252–53

More *Top Secret Recipes*® from

Todd Wilbur